WHEN POWER
CORRUPTS

Lionel S. Lewis

WHEN POWER CORRUPTS

Academic Governing Boards in the Shadow of the Adelphi Case

Transaction Publishers
New Brunswick (U.S.A.) and London (U.K.)

Library of Congress Catalog Number: 00-037389
ISBN: 0-7658-0031-4
Printed in the United States of America

Library of Congress Cataloging-in-Publication Data

Lewis, Lionel S. (Lionel Stanley)
    When power corrupts : academic governing boards in the shadow of the
    Adelphi case / by Lionel Lewis.
        p. cm.
    Includes bibliographical references (p.) and index.
    ISBN 0-7658-0031-4
    1. Adelphi University—Administration—Case studies. 2. Adelphi University—Faculty—Case studies. 3. Teacher-administrator relationships—New York (State)—Garden City—Case studies. 4. Diamandopoulos, Peter.
    I. Title.

LD25.8 .L49 2000
378.747'245—dc21   00-037389

Contents

Acknowledgments

Help to speed along completion of this project—from providing boxes of documents to giving valuable suggestions about the use to which these were being put—came from many quarters. Philip G. Altbach, Boston College; the Baldy Center for Law and Social Policy; Saul B. Cohen, Board of Regents of the University of the State of New York; Amy Gladstein and Beth M. Margolis, Gladstein, Reif & Meginniss, Attorneys at Law; Judge Barbara Howe, Supreme Court of the State of New York; Jonathan Knight, B. Robert Kreiser, and Michael Mauer, American Association of University Professors; Frederick P. La Forge and Allyn B. Skinner, my research assistants; Ann W. Lewis; Joel I. Nelson, University of Minnesota; and Sandra Walton, Ruben Salazar Library, Sonoma State University have been generous with material support, time and advice, and I am grateful. If I have forgotten others, I apologize; the obligations incurred in writing *When Power Corrupts* extend far beyond my power to remember and cite.

This book is dedicated to the others of the Lewis pride: June, Dorothy, Jack, Bernice, and Barbara.

Preface

The findings of this case study, which focuses on the governing board/administrative-faculty relationships at Adelphi University, have implications for a significant number of the 3,600-plus institutions of higher learning across the United States. They run counter to a number of commonly held assumptions about the putative power of faculty and about governance in American colleges and universities wherein lay governing boards have unlimited power, and faculty have been accorded a good deal less power than is believed.

In spite of the fact that academic administrators are appointed by and are the agents of trustees (not representatives of faculty or student interests), the latter who have complete authority over institutional policies, are hardly positioned to govern effectively. They are usually dependent on those whom they have appointed. Administrators may not only influence who is asked to join a board, but can also largely determine the content of the information boards receive—and so significantly shape their decisions. Moreover, because most members of lay governing boards know little about academic life, when faced with a decision, they must often defer to academic administrators, or acquiesce to a president's suggestions, whether perspicacious or not. Their judgments may be neither well informed nor, in the end, sound if the information provided is seriously flawed. A number of instances of this were found in this research, suggesting that the institution of self-perpetuating lay boards in American higher education may not be the best way of governing colleges and universities.

At the same time, one often hears that faculty with full-time positions, most of whom are protected by a permanent appointment (tenure), are free to do pretty much as they please. Some faculty in some prestigious institutions have considerable latitude in how they spend much of their time. Yet, what they can do is clearly circumscribed by governing boards and the administrators they appoint, those who control institutional resources.

Although ostensibly professionals, in many ways faculty seem to have no more autonomy than most employees in organizations. Indeed, despite many claims to the contrary, faculty in most American colleges and universities, with the exception of issues surrounding faculty-student relationships, have little power. It is not faculty who control how money is spent and who spends it, which programs will grow and which will wither.

When Power Corrupts details the struggle for control between, on the one hand, the Board of Trustees and administration and, on the other hand, the faculty at Adelphi University in Garden City, New York between 1985 and 1996 which culminated in the removal of the Trustees by the New York State Board of Regents. The new (New York State-appointed) Trustees then dismissed the President. What occurred at Adelphi is used as a backdrop for discussing the imbalance of power and governance in American institutions of higher learning.

Relying heavily on a thorough examination of the nearly 8,000-page transcript of the hearings conducted by the Regents, the eleven volumes of exhibits submitted by both the Board of Trustees and the faculty, hundreds of documents collected from several organizations —the American Association of University Professors, law firms representing the parties, and library archives—and by individuals on both sides of the conflict, and interviews with some of the principals, what was found suggests that academic administrators are more in control of governing boards and faculty than is generally recognized.

The prolonged conflict at Adelphi is not a deviant case, but an extreme and telling example of the perilous effects of the disparity of power in academia. At a minimum, what is most harmed by such rancor, perennial or short-lived, are teaching and students—always students.

1

Introduction

On Power in Academia

Poets, politicians, and philosophers have over time reminded us of the dangers of excessive power.[1] Shelley in one of his better-known poems, *Queen Mab,* an attack on monarchy, writes: "Power, like a desolating pestilence, pollutes whate'er it touches."[2] William Pitt observed that "unlimited power is apt to corrupt the minds of those who possess it."[3] Fearful of the danger that it had to curb or destroy liberty, Lord Acton's observation that "power tends to corrupt, and absolute power corrupts absolutely"[4] has become almost proverbial. Leibniz concluded that "those who have more power are liable to sin more; no theorem in geometry is more certain than this."[5] This book examines the validity of these related propositions in an academic setting. It shows the harmful effects of the imbalance of power between, on the one hand, a mostly vulnerable faculty and, on the other hand, an institution's governing board and administration with the force of law and custom and all of the school's resources on their side.

The story is an extreme example of the deleterious effects of the disparity of power in academia. The series of events examined are the consequence of three distinguishing characteristics of American higher education: first, a lay governing board has almost unlimited power, but only limited knowledge of the college or university in its charge. Second, faculty have relatively little formal power in setting both an institution's academic and nonacademic agenda—from establishing departments and degree programs to deciding what constitutes a major field of study, even to approving a policy to permit sororities and fraternities on campus. To further their influence, what faculty believe their most effective weapons, moral suasion and resistance, often come to nothing. Third, in no small part in how they allocate resources and the information they provide the governing board, academic administrators pretty much control college and university campuses.

This is an analysis of what happened at one institution over a decade; it is a case study. What is described is not represented as typical of academic life. There are approximately 3,600 colleges and universities in the United States, and surely the distribution of power in all of these is not identical. In most, faculty might have considerable say on a wide range of matters—for example, in the classroom, on the contents of syllabi, over the evaluation of students. Yet, in none do faculty have more power than the governing board and the administration. This should be evident from the preponderance of legal actions and media reports which leave little doubt that it is faculty who are mistreated by administrators or boards on American campuses; seldom is it the other way around. Proportionally, only slightly fewer dogs are bitten by people than administrators tripped up by faculty. A disgruntled pack of faculty may expose an errant academic administrator, but most who come to grief do so irrespective of what they have done to faculty or what faculty have done to them. This is surely true in the case at hand.

If not fully generalizable, what is chronicled here is a cautionary tale of how power arrangements and the pursuit of power in American institutions of higher learning might well contribute to diverting the attention of too many from the purposes of higher learning. Put another way, the uneven and somewhat unique distribution of power (compared to institutions of higher learning, say, in Europe) in American colleges and universities often leads to a significant number of highly educated individuals wasting an appalling amount of time and money that might otherwise be spent on teaching and learning, on educating students, and advancing scholarship and science.

The wrangling by faculty and board-appointed academic administrators over prerogatives and control is an important dynamic in institutions of higher learning, although it is seldom addressed by those who write about the various crises supposedly eviscerating contemporary higher education—the culture wars, the swollen bureaucracy, tenure, the neglect of teaching, political correctness, the frenzy to publish, vocationalism, the overuse of part-time faculty, the over-indulged faculty, over-indulged students, the under-indulged faculty, under-indulged students, and so forth. Yet, this matter has a longer history and deeper roots than any of these so-called crises. The never-ending battles are so common, they are more often than not seen as normal, one of the constants of academia. And in a sense they are. It is hardly surprising that they are taken for granted. Stories about some craziness in New York or Florida are quickly forgotten as the latest furor in Oregon or Massachusetts becomes the subject of debate: Was the president of the State University of New York at Stony Brook wise in rescinding a job offer and placing a moratorium on recruitment for the troubled English department or should she have allowed the faculty to continue feuding over whom to hire at the risk of self-destruction? Did the administration of Boston College receive a bona fide request for retirement from the faculty member with whom it had been quarreling for a number of years over her refusal to allow males to enroll in her courses or did it just unceremoniously cashier her?

Debates over how resources should be allocated—How large should the intercollegiate athletic program be? Indeed, should there even be an intercollegiate athletic program? Should there be a new performing arts center or should the funds be spent to improve professional programs in order to attract and hold more students? Why are faculty salaries lagging while class sizes continue to increase?—do not get much attention off campus unless an inexplicable or eye-catching episode finds its way into the mainstream media.

Who's in Charge?

This study begins with the premise that academic administrators, having been given authority by governing boards, hold a great deal more power in institutions of higher learning than faculty. When administrators and faculty disagree on institutional issues, outcomes are generally more in line with what the former than what the latter would like. To many who have some knowledge of how institutions of higher learning work, this might seem like a truism hardly worthy of note. Yet, a large number of the public, opinion leaders, and conventional wisdom hold that the opposite is true.

In recent years, the American professoriate has been mercilessly scapegoated for nearly all of the shortcomings of higher learning—from poorly educated students to budget shortfalls and ballooning costs. Indeed, the professoriate has long been an object of derision and complaint. Most of the criticism has been directed toward its commitment, effort, and competence.

Since at least the early 1960s, and with growing frequency, one hears the charge that faculty have usurped control of institutions of higher learning and have been running them for their own benefit without regard to the needs of students or the community at large. A great deal of the commentary on higher education has accepted and repeated without examination the erroneous opinion of David Riesman and his many students and followers that there was an expansion of faculty hegemony over governing boards and academic administrators following the Civil War that lasted for over 100 years, that moreover "the shape of American higher education is largely a response to the assumptions and demands of the academic professions."[6]

Although supported only by assertion and anecdotal evidence, Riesman's thesis is believed in many circles, having been most forcefully advanced by a number of present and former academic administrators. In 1964, Clark Kerr, while president of the University of California, first spoke then wrote of the faculty's "new sense of independence from the domination of the administration.... [M]uch administration has been effectively decentralized to the level of the individual professor.... So the professor too has greater freedom. *Lehrfreiheit*, in the old German sense of the freedom of the professor to do as he pleases, also is triumphant."[7]

George Dennis O'Brien, who served as president of both Bucknell University and the University of Rochester for nearly two decades, laments the emergence of "new-style universities" with their "dominating faculties," and asserts that he would like to see the "century of the faculty" replaced by a "century of management" in which there "will have to be some change in the nature, structure, and status of faculties."[8] In the preface to his collection of observations on contemporary higher education, O'Brien contends that "the research university revolution caused a tectonic shift in authority away from the president to the faculty.... Because the rise of the modern university is also the rise of faculties from subservience to authority, it would seem that it is faculty aims and faculty authority that will resolve the unsettled state of affairs."[9]

Frank Newman, who was president of the University of Rhode Island, attributes the untimely resignation of the statewide chancellor in Maine to the raw power of faculty: "What's the message?... It's that faculty are in charge, and if you try to make changes and force the issue, you talk yourself out of a job."[10]

Surely, most faculty would be surprised to learn that they had all this autonomy and control; they would be delighted if it were so. In light of all of this putative power, one might ask: Why are there so many instances of faculty wronged by the academic apparatchik, while, at the same time, given their boundless freedom and endless opportunities, why are there relatively so few instances of faculty bedeviling academic middle-management (e.g., deans), students, or others who make demands on them? Why do so few faculty neglect their responsibilities? To be sure, it is not always true that the abuse of power is a sign of its presence (and that the absence of abuse is a sign of little power) although this is often the case.

Notwithstanding what seems to be fairly apparent, the contention that the professoriate runs institutions of higher learning has gained considerable credibility in spite of the fact that during a good part of this century, most clearly in recent years, faculty have actually lost power to the distended bureaucracy and to a dismal academic labor market.[11]

Without question, for nearly half of the twentieth century—mostly between the late 1920s and early 1970s, with the exception of the more intense Cold War years[12]—the power of the American professoriate did marginally increase as the principles of academic freedom and tenure spread from one school to another across the country. These were especially good years for scientists and those with appointments in professional schools at research universities. While some administrative prerogatives may have diminished during this period, faculty never came close to wresting power from lay boards or academic administrators.

Upton Sinclair's description of academics early in the twentieth century clearly suggests vulnerability, not empowerment: "There are few more pitiful proletarians in America than the underpaid, overworked, and contemptuously ignored rank and file college teacher. Everyone has more than he—trustees and presidents, coaches and trainers, merchants and tailors, architects and building contractors, sometimes even masons and carpenters."[13]

In 1930, Abraham Flexner also characterized the American professoriate as "a proletariat, lacking the amenities and dignities they are entitled to enjoy."[14] Logan Wilson's 1942 observation of faculty, perhaps less harsh, is in no way contradictory: "Unlike many other professional intellectual workers, the professor is always an employee and has to conform to basic administrative controls common to all organized undertakings."[15] These are hardly descriptions of individuals with much authority or influence, or much of anything.

When the academic marketplace moved from a seller's market to a buyer's market in the early 1970s, most of the professoriate's gains in the previous decades in terms of autonomy (for example, to set limits on class size or to put in place funding to carry out research) and income began to erode, particularly for those not at top-ranked institutions. To a degree, some visible faculty with appointments at a small number of elite institutions, major research universities and well-endowed liberal arts colleges who had formed close relations with the state or private industry—with generously supported research programs—continued to be pretty much free from the oversight of academic administrators. The majority of faculty, however, saw their bargaining power plummet and their privileges decline. More and more faculty began to be hired on a temporary or part-time basis. Most of the American professoriate returned to its status of earlier times, and in many quarters is once again seen and treated as relatively powerless employees. To stem the tide, some faculty in the 1970s began to unionize. It is still unclear whether this has worked to their advantage.

To be sure, since World War II, few American campuses have been run by all-powerful (authoritarian, sometimes despotic) presidents (such as Charles William Eliot, Nicholas Murray Butler, or William Rainey Harper), a genus labeled "captains of erudition" by Thorstein Veblen in 1918.[16] Generally, the greater the prestige of a school, the less peremptory the administration. Yet, this hardly means that the American professoriate—through an extensive network of committees—has seized power from academic administrators.

In the best circumstances, there is a dual system of authority in American institutions of higher learning. At the center is a formal hierarchy with a chain of command that runs from the governing board through the administration to faculty and students. There is also a formal and informal network consisting of committees and other mechanisms to bring the professional expertise of the faculty into the decision-making process. Sometimes senior professors with reputations that extend beyond the campus[17] or with personal ties to administrative officers serve as unofficial sounding boards, and wield tangible power.

Whatever the formal or informal arrangements, there are few, if any, institutions of higher learning in the United States where the administration is bound by faculty recommendations. As a general rule, the deliberations and judgment of faculty are taken into account when they are asked for and when the administration chooses, surely when they are consistent with what the administration sees as the institution's needs and objectives. On occasion faculty can, and do, change the minds of administrators; the reverse is also true. As an example of the former, distinguished faculty members at distinguished institutions in a pique who threaten to resign sometimes get their way. Moreover, not all faculty believe that academic administrators have too much power. Unless its decisions and actions are so misguided, an administration can depend on a good number of faculty to routinely take its side.

Critics of putative faculty rule contend that protected by permanent appointments (i.e., tenure) after seven years of service, they are accountable to no one. Althouth tenure often works to protect faculty, there is no evidence to support this contention. American faculty do not and have never controlled life on campus or, in fact, even their own institutional careers. Since colonial times, formal power in American colleges and universities has been vested in lay governing boards that give a large part of their attention to fiscal matters and the conditions of the buildings and grounds, and hire like-minded senior administrative officers to look after an institution's day-to-day management.

At most, tenure gives a faculty member some control over his or her life. On the other hand, the province of college and university presidents is broad, and ranges from managing the budget and personnel, fundraising, and ceremonial duties, to convincing board members (and to a lesser degree the interested public) that they and their staff are contributing to the institution's success by maximizing favorable and minimizing unfavorable publicity emanating from campus that could impair these activities. All of this is best done when students, faculty, and others connected with the school are mollified, happy, busy, or in other ways distracted. (None of this contradicts the conclusion of Cohen and March that campus "presidents occupy a minor part in the lives of a small number of people. They have some power, but little magic. They can act with a fair degree of confidence that if they make a mistake, it will not matter much."[18]) The fact remains that American faculties have been and will continue to be subject to control by lay governing boards and academic administrators, those who control an institution's purse strings.

When focusing on academics in his analysis of "the special position of professional employees," Eliot Freidson makes this point with great clarity:

> In most if not all American colleges and universities the faculty does not have the authority to allocate the resources needed to advance its collective activities. Academic administrators, from department head on up, do have such authority: they decide not merely what individual faculty members will be paid and what the standard work load will be but also what faculty positions will be filled, which is to say, what courses can be taught competently, what disciplines will be staffed, what programs will exist, and what the curriculum itself can be. The faculty has the discretionary right to determine how those resources, once granted, will be put to use but not the right to determine how those resources are to be allocated in the first place....
>
> Committed to its disciplinary interests, a university department may wish to hire new staff in order to develop a new specialty that is, in its judgment, essential for an up-to-date program. Believing that other programs have a higher priority, the administration may refuse the resources necessary for hiring that new person and thus prevent an up-to-date program. A faculty may wish to institute a program composed of small discussion groups and tutorials by which each student would receive intensive attention and instruction, but since this would require hiring more staff, the administration may refuse the necessary resources and so preclude the possibility of employing such methods of teaching. In short, the professional staff seeks resources for the advancement of its work as it conceives of it, and management allocates resources according to its own view of priorities. There is a clear division of interests and power between the two.[19]

Collegial decision making is a vestige of the great medieval universities where there was a tradition of faculty control. In the Middle Ages in much of Western Europe, academic life was in the hands of societies of masters; there were no all-powerful governing boards or any standard system of state control. There was close to a true community of scholars. Although faculty spent considerable time engaged in meetings, administration, as we know it in the United States today, was nearly invisible. Higher education was self-governing, which allowed the faculty, as Haskins has noted, to escape "some of the abuses of a system which occasionally allows trustees or regents to speak of professors as their 'hired men.'"[20]

In the United States, with formal power and ultimate authority and control over resources, governing boards and their academic officers have been able to effectively thwart attempts of faculty to even approach true self-governance, to decide what rules will govern them. As Reece McGee has noted:

> All academic institutions except the most unabashedly tyrannical have some form of faculty government. Such structures are typically charged with determination of curriculum, degree requirements, committee structure, grading, standards of scholarship, and so on. Their authorizations, in other words, principally concern students. This is, indeed, a form of power, but it is not the power of self-determination, and it is amazing how rarely this distinction is enunciated. In most colleges, almost all authority to finally determine matters pertaining to the faculty lies with the board, president, and dean and not with the faculty themselves. Real power in academic institutions is the power over budget, for budget decisions determine who is to be hired and who is not and what he will be paid, what programs will be encouraged or shut off from further support, and what lines of endeavor will be rewarded. Perhaps only second in influence to the power over budget is the power to allocate time and space, and the authority to make these decisions also lies outside faculty purview since class loads, research leaves and offices, extra-classroom assignments, and so on are all administrative decisions.[21]

(In Europe, the latitude that was once faculty's has been greatly diminished.)

Regardless of the facts or what such knowledgeable observers as Flexner, Freidson, Haskins, McGee, Sinclair, Veblen, and Wilson have written, it is still widely believed that academic administrators spend much of their time doing the bidding of faculty. The reality is quite different: Budgetary decisions are made by governing boards, politicians in Sacramento, Albany, or Washington, D.C., and by academic administrators, certainly not by faculty. Ultimately, faculty owe their appointments to the institution's administration who promote, hire, and fire them on behalf of the governing board.

Salaries in Academia

If power were more equally shared between academic administrators and faculty as some insist, it might be expected that their rewards would be fairly similar. Obviously, the correlation is far from perfect, but power and economic rewards are related: those who have the most power in an organization are generally those who receive the greatest

TABLE 1.1
Median Salaries for Full Professors and Academic Administrators,# 1991-97

Title	Salary 1991-92	Salary 1993-94	Salary 1995-96	Salary 1997-98
Professor (U)	$65,190	$68,700	$73,610	$79,346
Professor(C)	$46,860	$50,080	$53,410	$56,969
Chief, Executive*	$95,500	$102,300	$114,298	$124,432
Chief, Academic**	$72,676	$79,796	$86,504	$92,000
Chief, Business***	$68,500	$75,620	$82,027	$89,000

It should be noted that salaries of administrators are for an 11-month year, while salaries for faculty are for a 9-month year. When comparisons are calculated on a monthly basis, the situation for university professors looks considerably brighter.

* Chief executive officer of a single institution.
** For example, dean of faculty, academic vice president, executive vice president, or provost.
*** Financial officer.

remuneration. Those with power can use it to bring about this outcome. On the assumption that this relationship between power and rewards holds in an academic setting, table 1.1, with figures drawn from the *Chronicle of Higher Education Almanac*, was constructed to compare salaries of full professors in universities(U) and colleges(C) with those of senior academic administrators.

The comparisons in table 1.1 show that between 1991 and 1997, senior academic administrators earned more than both college or university professors. The median salaries of presidents were over twice those of college professors, and the gap between the two grew during the 1990s, as the salaries of presidents increased faster than those of college professors (30 percent versus 22 percent) during this period. In 1991, the salaries of university professors were two-thirds of presidents; by 1997, the gap had widened slightly.

University professors made close to 90 percent of what chief academic officers made in 1991, and because their salaries did not grow as fast (22 percent versus 27 percent), a little less than this by 1997. College professors made 64 percent of what chief academic officers made in 1991. Because their salaries did not increase as fast, by 1997, they were earning only 61 percent of what chief academic officers made.

To the degree that power is positively related to rewards, these figures—although far from being definitive as they tell us nothing about variations within or between schools—lend support to the contention that academic administrators have more power than faculty.

None of this is to minimize the fact that, in many colleges and universities, faculty are relatively autonomous employees as long as they fulfill their routine duties without incident. The rights of faculty can be considerable, and include academic freedom, tenure, control over the curriculum, direction and control of the courses they teach, and some say in evaluating colleagues. If not too capricious, bizarre, ardent, or unsettling, their assessments of or relationships with students are seldom called into question.[22] At the same time, a great deal of what they do is subject to administrative approval; academic officers with the backing of the governing board almost always have the final word. For example, even supposedly inviolable tenure can be revoked if financial exigencies, as defined by academic administrators, require it.

As a rule, institutional by-laws make it clear that votes by faculty committees are strictly advisory; they can be, and now and then are, overturned by administrators and governing boards. The reverse is not true; it takes considerable effort on the part of faculty—usually intervention from someone off campus—to undo an action of a campus president. The decisions of academic administrators have more consequence for the lives of faculty than the decisions of faculty have for the lives of academic administrators. Further, and of great significance, the state has also worked to frustrate faculty attempts to control the conditions of their employment in that the courts have put the possibility of this becoming a reality further out of reach.

The Yeshiva Decision

In 1980, in what has become known as the Yeshiva Decision, the United States Supreme Court by a 5 to 4 margin upheld a court of appeals ruling that full-time faculty in private institutions of higher learning (in this case Yeshiva University) in essence hold supervisory and managerial positions.[23] The lower court had overturned a National Labor Relations Board's ruling that the opinions and actions of faculty when participating in academic governance are guided more by their professional values than by their individual interests, and therefore they cannot be said to be working with or carrying out the wishes of academic administrators. In short, within the meaning of the National

Labor Relations Act, faculty are professional employees, not management.

However, the Court's interpretation of the law was different. As it saw it, faculty "in effect, substantially and pervasively operat[e]"[24] institutions of higher learning.

In the majority's opinion, the professoriate's authority "in academic matters" is "absolute": it has extensive control over academic and personnel decisions; it effectively determines the "curriculum, grading system, admission and matriculation standards, academic calendars, and course schedules."[25] Moreover, the overwhelming majority of faculty recommendations with regard to the hiring and termination of colleagues, the awarding of tenure, the granting of sabbatical leaves, and promotions are implemented.

The case was brought to the Supreme Court in order to get a definitive ruling on whether or not faculty are entitled to the benefits of collective bargaining under the National Labor Relations Act. The Court concluded that they were not. The National Labor Relations Board had argued that "faculty participation in collegial decision making is on a collective rather than individual basis, it is exercised in the faculty's own interest rather than 'in the interest of the employer,' and final authority rests with the board." It was the Court's position that faculty were central to developing and enforcing policy and were free to use their independent judgment in overseeing colleagues:

> The controlling consideration in this case is that the faculty...exercise authority which in any other context unquestionably would be managerial.... To the extent the industrial analogy applies, the faculty determines...the product to be produced, the terms upon which it will be offered, and the customers who will be served.[26]

The Court acknowledged that the administration, with the approval of the board, has great power because it controls fiscal matters and formulates "general guidelines dealing with teaching loads, salary scales, tenure, sabbaticals, retirement, and fringe benefits."[27] Its decision, nonetheless, means that faculty at private colleges and universities are not covered by the provisions of the National Labor Relations Act, and thus do not have the right to bargain collectively. Central to the Court's decision was its rationale that the purpose of such an exclusion is to ensure an employer "the undivided loyalty of its representatives."[28]

The loss by faculty of this landmark ruling has had three additional consequences. First, it impedes the ability of faculty to unionize, to increase their power. Across the country since 1980, academic administrators at private institutions have used the Yeshiva Decision to challenge efforts of faculty to organize for the purpose of collective bargaining. Indeed, in some instances the power gained by faculty through collective bargaining has been reversed as courts have struck down union contracts as inconsistent with the Yeshiva Decision. Second, as noted by the Court's minority, it "removes whatever deterrent value the Act's availability may offer against unreasonable administrative conduct."[29] Finally, not only has it actually weakened the position of faculty, it, ironically, has worked to perpetuate the belief that faculty "formulate and effectuate"[30] academic policy, that is, that they have considerable power.

The Setting

This is a study of the administration of Peter Diamandopoulos at Adelphi University between 1985 and 1996. Adelphi University is located in Garden City, New York, forty minutes from Manhattan by commuter train. With academic-style brick buildings and expansive green spaces, the main seventy-five-acre campus has been described as exuding "a dignified serenity befitting a century-old institution with a proud past." During the Diamandopoulos presidency, it was rated by one national newspaper as America's safest campus.

However, appearance and reality are not always the same thing. Perpetual strife defined Adelphi during most of this period as much as a pastoral and orderly ambience. Throughout these years, there was considerable friction between faculty and administration, even as judged by the relatively permissive criteria of the academic world where discord, by energizing the participants, can become addictive and a way of life. The events at Adelphi in the 1980s and 1990s greatly exceeded these outsized standards. Adelphi was anything but serene.

The majority of those familiar with what happened at Adelphi between 1985 and 1996 are in agreement that there had been an egregious misuse of power by the Board and the administration over the eleven years of the Diamandopoulos presidency. What was initially restiveness on the part of a handful of campus activists, many of whom represented their colleagues in the Faculty Senate and in the faculty union, flared into a pitched battle between, on one side, an

overwhelming majority of Adelphi's faculty and, on the other, a uni-
fied Board of Trustees and the administration. (Some of the faculty
most supportive of the administration were the most distinguished.)

Confrontations with such enduring and explosive bitterness are not
common on American campuses. There may be considerable tension
between faculty and administration at a number of American colleges
and universities, but even when it erupts there are fewer outlandish
elements to catch the eye of the wider academic community, the media, and public officials as was true at Adelphi.

Before conflict escalates to the level it reached at Adelphi, it likely
has ended through mediation, marginalization, or the rout of one party,
most often part of the leadership of the meddlesome or dissatisfied
faculty. Even an academic administrator subject to a vote of censure
or no confidence by faculty is unlikely to be replaced or chastened by
a governing board. Occasionally a president under siege may take
early retirement or, consistent with Parkinson's Law, move to a better
position at another campus or to head a philanthropic, or some other
nonprofit, organization.

The all-out war at Adelphi cannot be viewed as something continually replayed across the country; its ferocity is quite unusual. In fact,
Adelphi is but one institution, and a claim cannot be made that events
there represents anything more than what occurred there between 1985
and 1996. Still, although what happened is not typical or important in
its consequences to higher education in America, the details of the
story illuminate a great deal about board/administrative-faculty relations and governance on American campuses.

The imbalance of power between, on the one hand, the lay board
and the administration and, on the other, the faculty at Adelphi is a
characteristic of all American institutions of higher learning. It is this
common feature that makes the Adelphi case relevant to American
higher education.

Some, if not all, elements of governance at Adelphi can be found
on most American campuses. The particulars of the upheaval at Adelphi
may not be representative and generalizable, but they illustrate how
this imbalance of power affects academic governance, how it sometimes works in colleges and universities. To characterize this peculiar
story as a deviant case (rather than an extreme case), erroneously
suggests that the imbalance of power evident at Adelphi is atypical on
American campuses. It is not.

While certainly uncommon, many implications of this story reach far beyond the Adelphi campus. Actually, it is the uniqueness of events that led to this study: the fact that the conflict was extreme and public produced a voluminous record, which provides a rare opportunity to examine closely and in depth the effects of the differential distribution of power in American higher education. It is for this reason that what happened can be fully recounted and understood, and sheds light on a situation not always recognized or acknowledged. The formal inquiry of the conflict at Adelphi affords us a suitable occasion to look at board/administrative-faculty tensions. The mass of materials produced allows for more than a glimpse of an educational institution in crisis.

That what occurred at Adelphi could ever occur is perhaps the best evidence that the American professoriate is relatively powerless, at least at the majority of American institutions of higher learning, and raises legitimate questions about college and university governance. That lesson could not be any clearer.

Faculty power in institutions of higher learning is not small or inconsequential around the country, or as we will see, even at Adelphi. At the University of Minnesota during much of the 1990s the faculty and the board of regents were constantly at odds over a number of issues, and after each battle tensions continued to increase until the former finally threatened to unionize. Faced with this prospect and pressure from prominent alumni, several leading members of the board felt it necessary to resign. Yet, because of outcomes such as this, it cannot be concluded that faculty have as much power as board members or academic administrators.

During the height of the conflict at Adelphi when the Faculty Senate asked for President Diamandopoulos's resignation in the fall of 1995, its operating budget was cut and it was forced to relocate its meetings. Late the next month, the Diamandopoulos administration temporarily cut off telephone service to the office of the faculty union. The union filed a grievance with the vice provost—the grievance was in effect filed against the administration with the administration—charging that the Faculty Senate was being prohibited from meeting in "suitable rooms," impeding its work. It also complained that eliminating the Faculty Senate's budget made it impossible to conduct its business. The vice provost ruled that since the union contract was "silent in regard to the use of University facilities and/or allocation of

money for faculty involvement and participation in University governance," the "alleged violation" of "the allocation of money" is "without merit and the whole grievance is denied."[31]

On the other hand, on December 4, the University filed a "unit
clarification" petition with the National Labor Relations Board seeking to decertify the faculty union, forcing the union, with its limited
resources, to get legal representation to defend itself. Three days later,
attorneys hired and paid by the University sent certified letters to
fifty-seven individuals, mostly disaffected faculty, warning that it would
sue them for defamation if they did not retract statements critical of
the Adelphi administration and issue a "letter of unconditional apol-
ogy."

To be sure, at Adelphi faculty were able to thwart harassment, and
faculty are generally successful elsewhere. But they are mostly on the
defensive, and it is not without cost. Thus, it would be fallacious to
believe that the actions of the Diamandopoulos administration at
Adelphi were nothing more than an aberration, that this is simply an
instance of something going very wrong in a basically sound system.

Adelphi, the School

A private institution with no religious affiliation, Adelphi University was chartered in 1896 as Adelphi College, which was the out-
growth of an academy located in Brooklyn. It was at first coeduca-
tional, but in 1912 it became a women's college. In 1929, it moved to
Garden City, Long Island. In its early years, it was the only college in
Brooklyn, and then on Long Island, to offer a full liberal arts curriculum. In 1946, the College again began admitting men.

Through its College of Arts and Sciences, Honors College, School
of Education, School of Management and Business, School of Nursing, Derner Institute of Advanced Psychological Studies, School of
Social Work, and University College, Adelphi offers bachelor and
graduate degrees in arts and sciences and in education, business, nursing, psychology, and social work.

With the growth of its graduate and professional schools, in 1963
Adelphi was granted the status of a university by the New York State
Board of Regents. Some instruction also takes place at two smaller
satellite branches in Manhattan and Huntington, Long Island. Peter
Diamandopoulos was Adelphi's tenth president. (Of the nine preced-

ing him, three had actually been acting presidents.)

Adelphi is poorly endowed: in 1985, the tuition as a percent of its total educational and general expenses was 84.2; in 1990, the figure was 81.9; in 1995, it was 95.5.[32] As will become clearer, it is of particular interest that between 1985 and 1995, the percentage of Adelphi's expenses funded by tuition markedly increased; there were large jumps between 1990 and 1991 and between 1991 and 1992.

Adelphi's national ranking among private institutions is sometimes in "the third tier" and sometimes in "the fourth tier." (It generally is placed somewhere in the third quartile to as far down as the twenty-fifth percentile among the over 200 national universities.)

In the late 1990s, the University was accepting roughly 70 percent of those who applied. Adelphi has always been a commuter school; over 90 percent of its students are from New York, a significant number of those from Long Island. Many attend part time.

The number of Adelphi's students and faculty is relatively small for a university. The school's size is not insignificant to the history of faculty-administrative discord that existed even prior to the Diamandopoulos years. In academic settings, and perhaps in other settings as well, the smaller the unit, the more likely contending parties will come to grief. This seems to lend support to the adage: strange things happen when the world gets small.

In several ways, Adelphi appears to be a fairly typical American liberal arts college. Its most popular majors have been business, nursing, and education. For most of its recent history, it has not been a school—not unlike most American liberal arts colleges—where students with a great passion for a true liberal arts education would be drawn. Its class sizes are relatively small; over half have fewer than twenty students. The student/faculty ratio has been a stable 12:1.[33] Adelphi's tuition for the 1998-99 school year was $14,420.

Peter Diamandopolous

Born in Crete in 1928, Peter Diamandopoulos earned his undergraduate and graduate degrees at Harvard University. He taught philosophy at Bates College, Swarthmore College, and Brandeis University (where he was also a dean) before being appointed president of Sonoma State University in California, a position he was forced to resign after incessant turmoil, the result of a prolonged, bitter battle with the faculty which culminated when he attempted to dismiss two dozen tenured faculty members (more about this in chapter 5). He describes the incident most benignly.

> Peter Diamandopoulos:
>
> Q: In 1983 were you fired from your position?
>
> A: No, I resigned.[34]
>
> Q: Were you asked to resign by the Board of Trustees?
>
> A: We had discussions with the leaders of the Board and I decided to resign.
>
> Q: After the discussions with the leaders of the Board of Trustees?
>
> A: Correct. (Testimony, pp. 118-19[35])

As a university president, Diamandopoulos could not be described either as a "headman"—cautious, amiable, and aimless; someone averse to risks—or a "leader"—someone with the ability to persuade others to welcome new initiatives. His management style at Sonoma and Adelphi was often described as autocratic; at times he appeared to be arrogant and at other times, condescending. He often resorted to coercion in his efforts to get others to do what he wanted.

The University of Chicago's William Rainey Harper, seen by many to be one of the most successful American university presidents, seems to have been of two minds regarding this type of leadership: "To be brutal [in saying no] may not be so good a policy at the time, but in the long run it probably pays."[36]

> In educational policy he [the president] must be in accord with his colleagues. If he cannot persuade them to adopt his views, he must go with them.... The president, if he has the power of veto, may stand in the way of progress, but he cannot secure forward movement except with the cooperation of those with whom he is associated.[37]

The second part of this message was consistently ignored by Diamandopoulos at Adelphi, and at Sonoma State University.

Diamandopoulos had a flamboyant touch, which some found charming and others found annoying. His detractors saw him as a bizarre charlatan, a shameless self-promoter. It was often said that he liked to describe himself as a philosopher-king. He pushed a grandiose scheme to make Sonoma State the "Brandeis of the West." While at Adelphi, he promoted a high-profile, hard-sell, and expensive advertising campaign in the *New York Times, New York Review of Books, Atlantic Monthly,* and *Harper's* boasting: "Harvard, the Adelphi of Massachusetts." The bombast sometimes appeared as full-page advertisements which seemed directed more at the cultural elite than at potential students. To prod the Adelphi community, he selected the affected slogan: "Because Good Is the Enemy of Great." This misleading apothegm was plastered across the campus on scores of posters.

None of what he conceived could accurately be called self-deception, as Diamandopoulos persuaded a number of others, most notably the Adelphi Board of Trustees, that his blueprint was practicable. Chapters 2 and 3 show how he went about doing this, and how easy it was.

Notes

1. As used here, power is defined as "the chance of a man or a number of men to realize their own will in a communal action even against the resistance of others who are participating in the action." (See *From Max Weber: Essays in Sociology* [translated and edited by H. H. Gerth and C. Wright Mills], New York: Oxford University Press, 1946, p. 180).
2. Percy Bysshe Shelley, *Queen Mab,* 1813, Oxford and New York: Woodstock Books, 1990, III, p. 40.
3. William Pitt, Speech: *Case of Wilkes,* 9 January, 1770.
4. See, G. E. Fasnacht, *Acton's Political Philosophy: An Analysis,* London: Hollis and Carter, 1952, p. 134. This well-known quotation is from a letter to Bishop Mandell Creighton.
5. Ibid.
6. Christopher Jencks and David Riesman, *The Academic Revolution,* Garden City, NY: Doubleday, 1968, p. 480.
7. Clark Kerr, *The Uses of the University,* Cambridge, MA: Harvard University Press, 1964, p. 44.
8. George Dennis O'Brien, *All the Essential Half-Truths about Higher Education,* Chicago: University of Chicago Press, 1998, pp. 28 and 133.
9. Ibid., pp. xii and xvi. He concludes his essay with the same theme: "If the twentieth century has been the century of *faculty,* the twenty-first will be the century of *administration*" (p. 227).

    In contrast to contemporary academic administrators, university presidents in the nineteenth and first half of the twentieth century favored faculty playing a prominent role in campus governance. Some examples:

    "It is the common custom for trustees to consign to faculties the determination of the requirements for admission and for the several degrees, of the methods and limits of instruction, and of the daily routine of duty for students and teachers, the

20 When Power Corrupts

administration of discipline, and the immediate supervision of the conditions of the academic life. Trustees should never interfere with matters once consigned to a faculty by statute or custom, unless in the way of inquiry or informal suggestion, or exercise any powers delegated to a faculty." (Charles W. Eliot, *University Administration*, Boston: Houghton, Mifflin, 1908, p.31).

"I insisted that the faculty should not be merely a committee to register the decrees of the president, but that it should have full legislative powers to discuss and to decide university affairs. Nor did I allow it to become a body merely advisory: I not only insisted that it should have full legislative powers, but that it should be steadily trained in the use of them." (Andrew Dickson White, *Autobiography,* volume 1, New York: The Century Co., 1905, p. 436).

"The trustees wisely refrained from interference with the faculty, to whom the government and instruction of the students was entrusted. The trustees made the appointments, it is true, but they were always guided by the counsel of the president and professors. They awarded the degrees, the scholarships and the fellowships, but only on the nomination and recommendation of the academic staff." (Daniel C. Gilman, *The Launching of a University*, New York: Dodd, Mead & Co., 1906, p. 49).

"Meanwhile the educational policies, including the standards of admission and graduation, programs of study and all matters pertaining to these or arising out of them, are settled as they should be settled, by the teaching staff organized into faculties, administrative boards, and standing committees.... The faculties must, of course, be legislative bodies and exercise legislative control over matters of educational policy falling within their several jurisdictions." (Edward C. Elliott, Editor, *The Rise of a University: 11, The University in Action,* [From the Annual Reports, 1902-1935, Nicholas Murray Butler], New York: Columbia University Press, 1937, pp. 382 and 417).

"Who should manage universities? Boards and presidents and faculty jointly. And how? By both formal and informal cooperation, and in the spirit of mutual confidence and respect." (Samuel P. Capen, "Who Should Manage Universities, and How?" in *The Management of Universities,* Buffalo, NY: Foster and Stewart, 1953, p. 21).

10. William H. Honan, "The Ivory Tower under Siege: Everyone Else Downsized; Why Not the Academy?," *New York Times (Education Life),* 4 January 1998, p. 46.
11. See Lionel S. Lewis, *Marginal Worth: Teaching and the Academic Labor Market,* New Brunswick, NJ: Transaction Publishers, 1996.
12. Lionel S. Lewis, *Cold War on Campus: A Study of the Politics of Organizational Control,* New Brunswick, NJ: Transaction Publishers, 1988.
13. Upton Sinclair, *The Goose-Step: A Study of American Education,* Pasadena, CA: published by the author, 1922, p. 390.
14. Abraham Flexner, *Universities: American, English, German,* New York: Oxford University Press, 1930, p. 208.
15. Logan Wilson, *The Academic Man: A Study in the Sociology of a Profession,* New York: Oxford University Press, 1942, pp. 120-21.
Wilson also writes:

Any random sample of institutions of higher learning would reveal some in which there is a trend away from faculty participation, others would show procedural stability, and still others moving in the direction of more self-government by their faculties. At present, there seems to be no clear indication of a general trend.... (p. 78).

The necessity for fundraising, for keeping a growing but loosely integrated structure from falling apart, and the deficiencies of scholars in collectively administering a complex organization have led to a semi-bureaucratic framework where most types of authority filter down from above. (p. 79).

16. Thorstein Veblen, *The Higher Learning in America: A Memorandum on the Conduct of Universities by Business Men*, New York: B.W. Huebsch, 1918.
17. To be sure, the greater a professional reputation, the freer one is to do as he or she pleases. The professional life of the great majority of faculty, however, is quite limited.
18. Michael D. Cohen and James G. March, *Leadership and Ambiguity: The American College President*, New York: McGraw-Hill, 1974, p. 205. This conclusion is based on their earlier observation that presidents "easily come to exaggerate the significance of their daily actions for the college," what they refer to as "a heroic conception of the consequences of action." (p. 204).
19. Eliot Freidson, *Professional Powers: A Study of the Institutionalization of Formal Knowledge,* Chicago: University of Chicago Press, 1986, pp. 150-51.
20. Charles Homer Haskins, *The Rise of Universities*, Ithaca, NY: Great Seal Books, 1957, p. 50.
21. Reece McGee, *Academic Janus: The Private College and Its Faculty,* San Francisco, CA: Jossey-Bass, 1971, p. 21.
22. See Ruth Shalit, "The Man Who Knew Too Much," *Lingua Franca*, Volume 8, Number 1, February 1998, pp. 31-40.
23. *United States Reports: Cases Adjudged in the Supreme Court at October Term, 1979*, Volume 444, "National Labor Relations Board v. Yeshiva University," pp. 672-706.
24. Ibid., p. 691.
25. Ibid., p. 676.
26. Ibid., p. 686.
27. Ibid., p. 675.
28. Ibid., p. 682.
29. Ibid., p. 705.
30. Ibid., pp. 682 and 695.
31. Memorandum from David Newton, vice provost for faculty/staff relations, 28 November, 1995, to Stephen Goldberg, president, Adelphi chapter of the AAUP. The administration giveth and taketh away: Earlier in the fall, President Diamandopoulos wrote to the chair of the Faculty Senate: "I have been informed by the senior vice president that your meeting last Friday was candid and constructive. I trust that you agree with his assessment, and that we can anticipate good progress on the University's common agenda. On the strength of your assurance to him that you will responsibly manage the monies allocated to the Senate for the pursuit of its work, I have instructed him to establish a viable operating budget for the Senate as soon as possible." (Memorandum from Peter Diamandopoulos, to Devin Thornburg 11 September, 1995). This stratagem and other demonstrations of Diamandopoulos's imperiousness seemed to animate rather than deter faculty as they continued to plague him.
32. Audited financial statements for years ending 1985-1995. Exhibit, P-303.
33. This figure has not changed much in recent years. In 1989-90, it was 12.20; in 1991-92, it was 12.47; in 1993-94, it was 11.97; and in 1995-96, it was 12.00. Exhibit, R-4P. (This refers to one of the exhibits [in this case, respondents' exhibit, number 4P] offered and accepted as evidence in the formal hearings before the panel of Regents.)

34. Years earlier Diamandopoulos denied that prolonged conflict with faculty at Sonoma State University, which, among other things, included his being censured three times, had anything to do with his leaving there. He told a newspaper reporter: "Rumor had it I was fired, forced to resign. No. I left. That's [the faculty vote] irrelevant, the faculty doesn't hire me. Or fire me." (Marilyn Goldstein, "2 Problem Schools, 2 Problem-Solvers: Diamandopoulos of Adelphi," *Newsday*, 6 June, 1986). In 1971, Diamandopoulos was also ousted as the dean of faculty at Brandeis University after he refused President Charles Schottland's request that he resign. ("President Fires Dean; Seeks Replacement," *The Justice* [Brandeis University], 12 January, 1971, pp. 1, 10, and 12). Apparently, Diamandopoulos did not hold a grudge. Adelphi awarded Schottland an honorary degree in 1986.
35. This refers to the page number in the sworn testimony in the formal hearings before the panel of Regents.
36. William Rainey Harper, "The College President," *Educational Record*, Volume 19, Number 2, April 1938, p. 180.
37. Ibid., p. 182.

2

The President and His Board I:
The Selection Process

Governing boards and college or university presidents are not truly independent of one another. Governing boards choose campus presidents. Only in some public institutions will someone become a member of a governing board over the objection of a college or university president. Faculty are not routinely and centrally involved in selecting members of governing boards and college presidents. Moreover, that governing boards and academic administrators generally act in concert, greatly diminishes the amount of power that faculty can acquire.

It is well understood that a governing board of an institution of higher learning selects the president and can be, to some extent, involved in overseeing the president's choices of other senior administrative officers. What is less well understood is that a college or university president—most particularly in private institutions of higher learning—can play a significant part in selecting and shaping the membership of a governing board. A president also greatly influences the decisions reached by a governing board.

Chapters 2 and 3 consider the consequences of the close alliance between governing boards and academic administrators for the governance of institutions of higher learning.

Misadventures at Adelphi: Introduction

In 1947, *Men Who Control Our Universities: The Economic and Social Composition of Governing Boards of Thirty Leading American Universities*[1] by Hubert Park Beck was published. Fifty years later, in

February 1997, after twenty-eight days of hearings before a subcommittee of the New York State Board of Regents, the full fifteen-member Board, with only one dissenting vote, recommended the dismissal of eighteen of the nineteen members of the Board of Trustees of Adelphi University.[2] The grounds for the Regents' action were threefold: that the remuneration in combined salary and benefits given to the University President, Peter Diamandopoulos was excessive, that the Board had been negligent in allowing the University to do business with companies in which some Trustees had a financial interest, and that the Board was derelict in overseeing, in general, the governance of the institution and, in particular, the performance of the President.

In his concluding comments, Beck strongly urged that institutions of higher learning amend their charters "to eliminate selection of trustees by co-option,"[3] the practice of "the filling of a vacancy by vote of the remaining board members."[4] If this had not been the practice at Adelphi, it is unlikely that the events that led to the Board of Regents' action would have occurred. Beck also recommended that there be a "restriction of the number of times a trustee could be reappointed to succeed himself."[5] Had this restriction been in place at Adelphi, a disaffected group—the Committee to Save Adelphi, which included University faculty, alumni, students and the parents of students, and former Trustees, administrators, and other employees—might not have been formed, and gone on to petition governmental authorities to initiate proceedings to remove the Trustees under Section 226 of New York's Education Law.

The Committee to Save Adelphi alleged that the Trustees were guilty of misconduct, neglect of duty, and the failure to see that the University effect its educational purposes. In New York, the law permits the Board of Regents to remove members of a governing board of any institution in the state, public or private, for any of these reasons. The rationale behind the law and the justification for such hearings is that the government bestows benefits on all colleges and universities in the form of tax exemptions and state and federal financial aid, and therefore some oversight and review by a public body is appropriate.

The thirty petitioners to the Board of Regents (twenty-three faculty, three former administrators, four former Trustees, five alumni/graduates, and four parents [these are not mutually exclusive categories] representing over 300 supporters of the Committee to Save Adelphi) had initially approached the Board of Trustees and requested that it investigate what they saw as mismanagement and the misuse of University assets.

The Trustees, in part because over half of the faculty with the closest ties to the Committee were or had been in the Faculty Senate (many of them as officers), which had been in a struggle with the President over issues of governance for a long period, dismissed the complaints out of hand. The only misconduct apparent to them was on the part of a handful of agitators in the Faculty Senate (and faculty union); they rejected the claims of the faculty firmly and publicly. On all counts, the Board backed the administration. In fact, it saw any criticism of Adelphi—except that of faculty—as baseless and malicious, and as an attack on it. Its initial response to earlier published reports suggesting that all was not well at Adelphi was to direct Diamandopoulos "to continue vigorously to take all steps necessary to advance the University towards the lofty and ambitious goals repeatedly articulated by the Board." In spite of mounting evidence that there were serious problems with the administration of Adelphi, the Board was satisfied that there were none. It would not look into the matter, there was nothing to it and it was not worth pursuing. Remedial measures were uncalled for and unnecessary.

In responding to the Committee's letter, New York's deputy commissioner for higher education and the professions for the State Education Department simply described the formal procedures for filing a petition with the Board of Regents. The Committee promptly took the necessary steps to press its charges with the Regents.

The case revolved around the issue of whether the Board of Trustees, which was charged with protecting the interests of the University, was truly remiss. Had the Board allowed the President to spend unlimited amounts of the University's assets for his own personal enrichment and self-aggrandizement, and had it abdicated its responsibilities to oversee the financial and academic management of the University?

There were additional allegations to bolster the Committee's case. Some University employees were said to have engaged in fraud, while others were defrauded. There were witnesses who could testify that at least one Trustee (the President) had details of thievery, and had turned a blind eye to the facts. In short, there was more to the record of mismanagement of the assets of the University.

The point was also made that many senior administrative positions were vacant and there was an unusually high turnover in others; this was put forth as an unmistakable sign of administrative bungling. Regardless of what was claimed, the Board of Trustees continued in its refusal to entertain the idea that there could possibly be any administrative disorder. Specifics about those Trustees doing business with the University—a clear violation of regulations governing conflict of interest—with considerable detail of the wrongdoings, came to the front in the complaint and petition to the Board of Regents.[6] Along with three others, the four most senior Trustees were at the center of the most serious allegations that the Committee to Save Adelphi lodged with the Board of Regents. One had been a Trustee for more than twenty-five years.

Co-Option

Long before Beck's study, the use of co-option as a method of appointing members to governing boards of institutions of higher learning had been questioned. In his analysis of American higher education in 1842, Francis Wayland suggested that trustees "should, if possible, be elected by some body out of themselves to whom they should be responsible. This would do much to secure efficiency and would leave opportunity to apply suitable correctives whenever they became necessary."[7] Wayland was also convinced that trustees "should be chosen for a term of time, and not for life. A body chosen for life is particularly liable to attacks of somnolence. Every thing in such a society tends in a remarkable degree to repose."[8] In some ways, this pretty closely describes what happened at Adelphi, even though it was eventually proven that a handful of Trustees were guilty of a great deal more than lethargy; they had become imprudently involved in the University's business affairs, arranging sweetheart deals for themselves and colleagues.

To be fair, it has not gone unnoticed that there are certain advantages to the process of co-option, namely, that it is a "dignified method which does away with the necessity of running for election or otherwise participating in partisan politics" and that it "guarantees a high degree of continuity and consistency in the policy of the board."[9] However, as will become evident, partisan politics very much permeated the Adelphi campus in spite of the uninterrupted ritualistic and lofty rhetoric about the higher purposes of higher learning and the intellectual needs of undergraduates. It should be added that even before they were embattled, some of the things a number of the Trustees said and did were hardly dignified.

Co-option is at the core of much of the tension between faculty, on the one hand, and the governing board and administration in American institutions of higher learning, on the other. The formal charter gives the board considerable power. It holds funds and property, selects the chief academic officer, and exercises overall jurisdiction.

In addition to what is agreed to be its principal function of fiscal oversight, the board is charged with establishing educational policy. It has broad powers; it frames the decisions that guide an institution's present and future. Through actions it might take with regard to financial matters and its general stewardship, it has ultimate control, the final word. The entire board, and most particularly its most active members, in meaningful ways can set the tone and direction of a college or university.

In short, governing boards have wide latitude to do as they wish. Whatever specific steps boards might take, co-option increases the likelihood that their new members will agree that they are pursuing the right course. Boards, after all, would not likely invite those who they know would differ with them to join them in membership. In light of this, the chances that a determined governing board could be deterred from doing something that faculty, rightly or wrongly, might oppose would surely decrease, while the strains between the two could well intensify.

Who's *Really* in Charge?

It is taken for granted that a governing board delegates the details of management to the administration, the president of which it directly appoints. One often hears that governing boards are fully in charge and that administrative officers follow their directions. Current and former members of governing boards often repeat this claim. Yet, this is largely a fiction; it certainly was not so at Adelphi.

For the most part, governing boards are naive about academic matters, do not commonly exercise power independent of what the administrators they appoint deem appropriate or necessary, and at times merely reiterate what they hear from academic administrators. Although it is almost universally and, not surprisingly, vehemently denied when it occurs, boards commonly become captives to those whom they have hired to carry out their wishes. This is more frequently the case than is recognized.

As a rule, the more secular interests of governing board members precludes their becoming immersed in academic culture. Because most board members lack a full understanding of academic culture and adequate time to master the arcane details needed to run a campus, more often than not, as it was observed more than seventy years ago, they operate "mainly as a rubber-stamping bureau for the policies and decisions of the president."[10] It is hardly surprising that board members would like to believe otherwise. Academic administrators are not inclined to disabuse them.

President Diamandopoulos with regularity, in fact, worked to perpetuate this misconception. In his report at the Board of Trustees meeting on September 22, 1993, he observed: "We have been all working together. We have one of the most distinguished governing boards in the country. I acknowledge and am responding to your view that we are going to achieve tremendous success in higher education. We have a lot of work to do."

In her testimony before the subcommittee of the Regents the chair of Adelphi's Board of Trustees attested to its control of the University, but what she describes in answering a series of questions contradicts her impressions.

Ernesta Procope:

Q: Who prepares the agenda for the meeting of the Board of Trustees?

A: Dr. Diamandopoulos prepares and shares it with me and asks me if I have any additions, corrections or deletions....

Q: And if a committee wanted to bring something to the attention of the Board of Trustees, how would the committee do that?

A: The committee would either—the committee chair would either contact me or Dr. Diamandopoulos. (Testimony, p. 752[11])

Q: So, I'm simply trying to ask, when you had these series of resolutions, and I believe you told me that it was the President who drafted them, not the Board, but the Board signed off on them—

A: He would discuss it with me and I would tell him, put it in writing, let me see it, let me take a look, he'd fax it to me, I'd take a look, if I had any comments I'd make them, send it back to him.

Q: So you accepted this at face value, his comments about being the center of educational innovation?

A: Yeah.

Q: Or being nationally recognized as such?

A: Yeah. (Testimony, p. 1341)

Q: Well, first of all, to establish what the document is, it's a copy of a speech the President will be delivering to the faculty at 3:30 and which he is sending to the members of the Board of Trustees. It strikes me as a for-your-information piece. In the fourth paragraph of page three, he speaks of a pretty significant scholarship program, $12,000 per year for those with certain grades, with presidential scholarships, et cetera. Now, it does strike me that this is an important policy issue, with not only academic implications but financial implications. So you're telling us that you did not discuss this within the Board or within the Academic Committee reporting to the Board, insofar as you know?

A: I can't recall this item being discussed specifically. (Testimony, pp. 1360-61)

It would appear that governing boards do something less than govern, and that campus presidents do a great deal more than simply preside and manage.

Whether a board or the campus president is truly in charge of a campus, a more important point is that the faculty is not. Faculty are not as a rule even represented on the board. Administrators are responsible for faculty, not to faculty. Management is very much in the hands of a president and his staff. When there are conflicts on matters or values between faculty and administrators, the former are vulnerable. Faculty are very far from being autonomous since control of the allocation of resources is in the hands of administrators.

Faculty may or may not be consulted either on broad educational issues or on more narrow, parochial policies that affect their salaries, teaching loads, fringe benefits, and the like. It has long been recognized that this arrangement has worked to the great detriment of faculty, and certain positive developments in higher education: "The American college both as an institution and in its entire personnel is immature, even childish; its state of dependency on a lay governing board [an inviolate theme which will be developed in some detail] makes for timidity and subserviency in the faculties and for tyranny in the executives."[12]

One consequence of their inability to press their interests with much success is that faculty not only are often seen, but have come to see themselves, as simply employees. In the eyes of a large proportion of the professoriate and the public, the academic calling has become simply a career. As Richard Hofstadter has noted, the fact that governing boards are by law the college or university "has hampered the development of organization, initiative, and self-confidence among American college professors, and it has contributed, along with many other forces in American life, to lowering their status in the community."[13]

Regretfully, many would say, the most visible and discordant "development of organization" on many campuses has been the movement toward unionization. As the administration and Board of Trustees of Adelphi University saw it, much of the turbulence that was frustrating their plans and putting the institution at risk was the result of the treachery of a handful of union troublemakers. Acting on this assumption, in the 1990s they spent a great deal of time, energy, and money in an effort to decertify the faculty union.

For their part, the more beleaguered they felt, the more inclined faculty were to turn to the union to keep them out of harm's way. The more faculty committed themselves to the labor union model of academic governance, the more academic authorities moved against them —and threatened them. This cycle of action and counteraction set Adelphi on a disastrous course.

Packing the Board

As a general rule, faculty and governing boards have little contact, and this was certainly the case at Adelphi. With the governing board and faculty pretty much isolated from one another, President Diamandopoulos was free to interpret the needs of Adelphi and to run the campus as he saw fit. He surrounded himself with a number of, by conventional academic standards, relatively well-paid sycophants, appointing to his administration too many others, who like himself, were academic mediocrities lacking in scholarly accomplishments, sound judgment, and a modicum of respect for a faculty who had a much stronger commitment to teaching than to research. The primary criteria for appointment and advancement in the Diamandopoulos administration were flexible ethics and intractable public loyalty.

Having published very little—nine definitions or biographical sketches of one or two columns each in the *Encyclopedia of Philosophy,* one paper of nine pages in an edited volume, and fifteen book reviews—Diamandopoulos had almost no scholarly record or reputation. Notwithstanding the lack of perceptible intellectual achievement, he convinced himself and others that besides being wise and good he was a scholar of original and great ideas. He even believed that comparisons between himself and Socrates were apt.[14]

Before long, aside from faculty critics, he encountered little resistance to this pretense, as he had been able to load the Board with individuals who, without reflection, accepted the image he cultivated and projected of a polymath, and they were keen to support him and his agenda. Most Trustees were overwhelmed and easily manipulated. As the years went by, fewer faculty were impressed by his manners than were intimidated by his nefariousness and vindictiveness.

To members of the Board, many with business backgrounds, Diamandopoulos's extravagances on expensive automobiles, trips to Europe to collect art (the faculty spread rumors that his purchases included works by Picasso, Calder, and Miro) and visits to his vineyards in Crete, membership in three exclusive private clubs (the Links Club, the Union League Club, and the University Club), and an upscale condominium on East 72nd Street in Manhattan affirmed the cosmopolitan manner he affected. (It should be noted that almost all of this, including the dues to the three clubs, was paid for by the University, as were extensive renovations and furnishings in the apartment, for which Diamandopoulos was given an option by the Trustees to purchase at a greatly reduced price.) Apparently the life-style of the college president that emerged from the Gilded Age caricatured by Upton Sinclair is obviously one that Diamandopoulos believed befitted him:

> The college president has acquired enormous prestige in American capitalist society; he is a priest of the new god of science, and newspapers and purveyors of "public opinion" unite in exalting him. He receives the salary of a plutocrat, and arrogates to himself the prestige and precedence that go with it. He lives on terms of equality with business emperors and financial dukes, and conveys their will to mankind, and perpetuates their ideals and prejudices in the coming generation. It is a new aristocracy which has arisen among us, and they all stand together, they and their henchmen and courtiers, against whatever forces may threaten.... We shall find it worth while to turn over the pages of "Who's Who in America," and see what these mighty ones of the earth think of one another, and what they do to flatter one another's pride, and to keep their own order in the public eye.[15]

To be sure, some members of governing boards may hold a less majestic view of academic administrators. This was evident in the reaction of the banker and patron of the arts, Seymour Knox, who as chair of the State University of New York at Buffalo's council had been central to bringing Martin Meyerson to the school, on hearing of the latter's decision to move to the presidency of the University of Pennsylvania:

> "I feel like a crumb-bum," he complained. "Yesterday, in Philadelphia, I ran into an old friend, Bill Day, who is now chairman of the Penn board of trustees. Was he gloating! God, it was awful. I felt like he'd stolen my cook."[16]

Yet, seeing a campus president as someone not quite as exalted does not necessarily make it any less likely that a board and a president can work together to make decisions they jointly favor regardless of the wishes of faculty.

Many Board members could not but be flattered and pleased by Diamandopoulos's characterization of them:

> It [the reclamation of Adelphi's philosophy of education] implies a strong and responsible governing board—one like the Adelphi Board of Trustees, a true governing board comprising enlightened men and women who constantly judge the ideas and ideals of the academy and who are deeply committed to the significance of education for the nation's future prosperity and achievement. This Board views itself as the authoritative agency responsible for the enactment of the University's educational mission.

> It is the Board that insists on the husbanding of resources, [through] their wise investment...and above all on fostering educational practices of the highest intellectual seriousness and boldness. The health of the University and its ability to educate today's students for the world of tomorrow depends absolutely on this commitment and on this enlightened and authoritative leadership.[17]

If this description were even close to reality, the New York State Board of Regents would not have found cause to remove the Adelphi Board of Trustees.

Fellow Traditionalists

During his tenure, the President, who was himself a member, was able to recruit to the Board of Trustees, which varied in size between eighteen and twenty-five, some academic types who shared his view that a good part of the curriculum for undergraduate students, regardless of their interests, must include the study of the philosophical, historical, literary, and cultural bases of Western civilization, most particularly American democracy. Trustee Donald Kagan elegantly and succinctly summed up this position: "The general education of the student...[is] a civic necessity. I think that the nation needs to have a population that has a proper education." (Testimony, p. 6079).

This traditional view and approach to education was inaugurated at Adelphi by what was called the Core Curriculum, a program that was justified by the argument that "one cannot claim to be educated without the command of a broad range of general ideas and an appropriate understanding of their implications."

The Core Curriculum's goal was straightforward: to provide students "with a vantage point from which to judge ideas as established by the thought of the Enlightenment and by the reactions to the Enlightenment, particularly as these powerful intellectual currents have influenced or served to shape modernity." It is assumed that in the end, after spending a significant portion of their undergraduate studies examining how our heritage has shaped present-day knowledge, students would have "developed a moral disposition and a self-critically ethical outlook."

> The Adelphi Core Curriculum is a multifaceted, four-year study of our modern age. We have chosen this focus because we believe it best enables a profound intellectual engagement for all Adelphi students of the sort envisioned in our philosophy of education.... [It] immerses the student in the world as we know it through a mandatory freshman sequence in "The Modern Condition and Its Origins."... In a culminating seminar on "Values and Actions," the Core Curriculum brings the whole of the student's learning to bear on meaning in his or her life, exploring the ethical dimensions of choice in the inescapable arenas of personal and public action.[18]

Given the behavior of the faculty and administrative leadership at Adelphi, this fanciful description might seem somewhat ironic. Yet, in the abstract it nonetheless is admirable, even in light of the fact that Adelphi's initiative here was considerably less original than the administration claimed. Similar programs implemented in the largely unsuccessful attempt to engage a significant number of undergraduates in the world of ideas, to more broadly educate them, can be found on hundreds of campuses across America.

The debate over whether or not the return to core curriculums truly benefits students, many of whom have little interest in serious education and such programs, has divided the academic community for decades. Behind the belief that a liberal education could only do good is the conviction that there is a body of knowledge that students should share if they are to become members of a vital academic community, the local and the more general, and that those who do not have some familiarity with it are not truly educated.[19] This view has as many opponents as champions. An early and often repeated criticism has been "that no one who possesses this much-desired culture—I am thinking of something much more substantial than the mere polish of a gentleman—has obtained it during the specified years of college. The idea that anything approaching a general education can be crammed down in four years of college, certified by an A.B., and enjoyed ever after without further effort, is the greatest impediment to the growth of American culture."[20]

Contemporary defenders of what has lately been referred to as the Western canon, like President Diamandopoulos, have in the 1980s and 1990s been frequently subject to ad hominem verbal abuse; it is not uncommon to hear them unfairly referred to as elitists, reactionaries, and even racists. Such attacks have reinforced their worst fears that higher education and rationality, and ultimately Western civilization, are truly endangered. They have naturally also sparked a fierce response. The counteroffensive has been fostered by the belief that not only are the truths at the foundation of American democracy not being taught to undergraduates, but that a left-leaning agenda is unabashedly being pushed by too many faculty on too many campuses. Faculty have become propagandists, academic administrators are weak-willed puppets, students are being brainwashed, and America's freedoms are being eroded.[21] An essay by Adelphi honorary Trustee William Simon is representative of the sentiment that faculty must be called to account for these wrongs.

A few months ago, Yale University returned a $20 million gift from alumnus Lee Bass rather than honor his request that the money be used for a course of studies in Western civilization. The incident spoke volumes about the intellectual and moral bankruptcy that has swept the U.S. academic community.

Yale is...strapped for cash.... Yet, the school apparently would rather turn its back on $20 million than offend the forces of "political correctness" and offer a course in the civilization that gave it birth....

The gift and its purpose were clearly announced in 1991.... Then, once the check was cashed, Yale began to back away from its promises, goaded by faculty who are openly hostile to a course of study celebrating the achievements of Western civilization....

Mr. Bass asked to review the faculty appointments made under his gift. The University responded with cries of outraged virtue.... Yale announced his gift would be returned....

The Bass episode is symptomatic of a wider sickness that is infecting institutions of higher learning across the country. The hostility toward Western civilization..., the practice of invoking the sacred cow of academic freedom as a cover for hypocrisy and irresponsibility—all are evidence of an increasing tendency to subvert true learning by replacing intellectual goals with political ones.

At Harvard, for example, radical faculty members are outraged at the prospect of having conservative columnist George Will teach a class as a visiting professor of government this fall....

When such professors speak of "tolerance," they mean courses like "Introduction to Gay and Lesbian Studies," to be offered next spring to undergraduates at Dartmouth College....

Make no mistake: The activist professors who control many of our universities are openly contemptuous of America and its way of life, and are determined to use the classroom to overturn it. To this end, they promote distorted images of our Constitution, our leading historical figures, and our achievements as a civilization. Textbooks and lecture halls are used to disseminate their point of view. And anyone who takes issue with it...is subjected to scurrilous attacks....

Unless universities begin to reform themselves, and work to turn their students into informed citizens of a free society—not partisan zealots formed in the image of a radical faculty—their standing in the eyes of the public will continue to decline.

And alumni and donors will increasingly withhold their support.[22]

A trustee who would make a public declaration portraying higher learning and the professoriate so inaccurately and unfavorably, would probably not have much respect for either, or be someone sympathetic to faculty autonomy or shared governance.

Fortunately, the divide at colleges and universities has not been as wide, deep, or dangerous as Simon would have his readers believe. In fact, campuses have not been overrun by swarms of evangelists of the Left. Nonetheless, a number of accomplished and serious academics have become convinced of this. They see name calling, the infringement of individual liberties to further minority interests, and other manifestations of intolerance on campus as a great danger. In their minds, all of this is also part of a larger problem, namely, that since the late 1960s rationality and objectivity have been in decline, and ideology masquerading as scholarship has steadily and firmly become a recognizable part of the academic landscape. As a result, some, most especially faculty from the humanities, have redoubled their effort to defend the faith by banding together in a body called the National Organization of Scholars. Four members of the 1997 Board of Trustees of Adelphi University—Peter Diamandopoulos, Donald Kagan, Hilton Kramer, and John Silber—were active in this group.

It is understandable that those Trustees not current with the issues academics debate (as Simon was satisfied he was) would defer to these four who certainly seemed to have the credentials of men of ideas—two philosophers who were university presidents, a distinguished Ivy League historian, and an art critic and the publisher and editor of an ideological periodical which some have characterized as an intellectual magazine—and eagerly embrace the one side of the academic controversy that was so positively presented to them. The assumptions and conclusions of the uncompromising position they represented were used to bolster President Diamandopoulos's push to advance some academic programs at the expense of others, regardless of the financial risks to Adelphi whose budget was so heavily dependent on student tuition.

Although it is unusual for members of governing boards to become involved in academic matters generally the concern of faculty and academic administrators, on occasion these fellow traditionalists did. Trustee Hilton Kramer even helped recruit faculty. Maurice Cowling describes his invitation: "When I was retiring from Peterhouse in 1993, I was approached by Mr. Hilton Kramer, the editor of the *New Criterion* of New York, to inquire whether I would like to be a visiting professor at Adelphi University of which he was a Trustee."[23]

Before he was formally on the Board, Donald Kagan's advice was sought on personnel matters:

Donald Kagan:

A: During that period, President Diamandopoulos on occasion asked me to recommend to him talented people that might be useful at Adelphi, faculty or administrative roles, and so I did recommend to him perhaps five or six people over that period of time. (Testimony, p. 5953)

Kagan as dean of Yale University and John Silber as president of Boston University, who had earned national reputations in academic circles and the distrust of some faculty by their sometimes heavy-handed efforts as administrators to impose a more structured curriculum on students and faculty, were, through the efforts of President Diamandopoulos, added to the Board, and were also over-represented on its committees.

John Silber:

A: There had been prior discussions of it [joining the Board], personally. James Byrne had talked to me about it many years earlier, and Peter Diamandopoulos had talked to me about it.

Q: Because President Diamandopoulos has testified that he and Chairman Byrne came to meet you to ask you to become a member of the Board of Trustees.

A: Well, I had met with them in Boston on several occasions prior to 1989, and one of those meetings may have been one in which they asked me. (Testimony, pp. 1542-43)

A: At the time that Peter took it, the University, Adelphi, was in deficit, and it was not at all clear that anything could save it from bankruptcy.... It became very interesting as I saw him build the Board and turn that University around. (Testimony, pp. 1543-44)

Q: Can you tell me, Dr. Silber, of the eight committees [including the Executive Committee, Advisory Council, Finance Committee, Trustee Affairs Committee, Investment Committee, Academic Affairs Committee, Shadow Advisory Committee for Labor Relations] that you are on of the Board of Trustees, how many meet on the morning of the Board of Trustees meeting? (Testimony, p. 1579)

Donald Kagan:

Q: Do you recall when you were first invited to join that Board?

A: Not precisely, but sometime after I received the honorary degree [from Adelphi] President Diamandopoulos asked me if I would serve in that capacity....

Q: What, if any, contacts had you had with President Diamandopoulos in the intervening period [before agreeing to serve on the Board]?

A: I believe there were two social events, he simply invited my wife and me down to New York for dinner on two occasions. (Testimony, pp. 5951-52)

In fact, President Diamandopoulos recruited most of the members of the Board. Here are parts of his testimony on this matter:

Peter Diamandopoulos:

Q: Did you recommend Mr. Krasnoff to the Board, sir?

A: Yes, ma'am, proudly so....

Q: Did you recommend Mr. Damadian to the Board, sir?

A: Mr. Damadian. Dr. Damadian. He's a physicist and an M.D. Dr. Damadian —

Q: I just asked you if you recommended him to the Board, sir.

A: Yes.

Q: Did you recommend Robert B. Friedman to the Board, sir?

A: Yes....

Q: Did you recommend Mr. Hilton Kramer to the Board, sir?

A: Yes....

Q: Did you recommend Mr. Kulukundis?

A: Kulukundis.

Q: Thank you for pronouncing it, sir. Did you recommend him?

A: Yes....

Q: Did you recommend Dr. Burke to the Board, sir?

A: Dr. Karen Burke, yes.

Q: And is she related, in any way, to any other member of the Board, sir?

A: She's the wife of Dr. Goulandris. (Testimony, pp. 504-507)

George Lois:

A: He [Diamandopoulos] asked me to join the Board. I'll never understand why I did it, because I don't really have much time to do anything, including see my grandchildren. But I was encaptured [sic] and enthralled by his ethos, and by his attitude and by his—I was totally captivated by his attitude about life and education in general. So I kind of reluctantly said I would, and I dove right in. (Testimony, p. 2388)

This was not a Board likely to take issue with much of what Diamandopoulos represented as a course of study that was sound, feasible, and necessary.

On the face of it, President Diamandopoulos's fancy which would require that all undergraduates be at least exposed to, or at best well-grounded in, an education emphasizing the liberal arts and sciences seems to make good sense. To a number of thoughtful individuals, on and off campus, too many college graduates are woefully ignorant about their heritage and culture, and do not understand basic scientific concepts or principles. Also, finding Trustees who would support this tack also makes sense; it would be unrealistic to expect Diamandopoulos to seek out more than a few, if any, individuals who were convinced that students already waste too much of their time studying subjects with little practical value.

At the same time, to plunge ahead with the plan as if there were no resistance by students, parents, and the public to that which is not vocational, professional, or technical education, is to ignore the sweep of American educational history; since the 1960s the percentage of students pursuing degrees in business, communications, physical therapy, nursing, and the like has mushroomed, while those majoring in, for example, classics, history, languages and literature, and philosophy have plunged. Whether or not one finds it disheartening, the facts are quite clear:

> Humanities represent a sharply declining proportion of all undergraduate degrees. Between 1970 and 1994, the number of B.A.s conferred in the United States rose 39 percent. Among all bachelor's degrees in higher education, three majors increased five- to ten-fold: computer and information sciences, protective services, and transportation and material moving. Two majors, already large, tripled: health professions and public administration. Already popular, business management doubled. In 1971, 78 percent more degrees were granted in business than English. By 1994, business enjoyed a four-fold advantage over English and remained the largest major. English, foreign languages, philosophy, and religion all declined. History fell, too. Some fields plummeted. Library science shrank to near extinction, from 1,013 B.A.s to 97. On the Preliminary Scholastic Aptitude Test, only 9 percent of students now indicate interest in the humanities....

> The most authoritative, trusted study of the subject (a yearly poll of college-bound high-school graduates) reveals that in 30 years a total flip-flop has

occurred in the proportion of freshmen entering college who expect their higher education to enhance future job security and ensure high-wage employment (greatly increased) versus those who want to develop values, form a broader social vision, experiment with varied forms of knowledge, and formulate a philosophy of living (greatly decreased).[24]

In short, the authorities at Adelphi seemed blind to what was obvious to most of the reading public: "In 1968, more than 21 percent of all of the bachelor's degrees conferred in America were in the humanities; by 1993, that number had fallen to about 13 percent. The humanities now must struggle to attract students, many of whose parents devoutly wish they would study something else."[25]

As lamentable as some might find it, it is doubtful (or at least it is not at all clear) whether even financial incentives in the form of liberal scholarships (offered by Adelphi, which, in fact, it could not really afford), could attract many students. To the great majority of American undergraduates (and their parents), immersion in the liberal arts is not the most direct path to a career. The Committee to Save Adelphi alleged in 1995 that "two thousand invitations for a luncheon, sent to prospective honors students, yielded a total of six attendees."

Diamandopoulos's blueprint also seems to have been unmindful of the level of culture of the American public, those with or without college degrees. To grasp this, all President Diamandopoulos needed to have done was listen carefully to some of his own Board members.

George Lois:

Q: I have some questions about the work of the Development Committee, which you are listed as being on in the year 1995.

A: Oh, you're back to the Development Committee, huh? I don't think you'll get me. I'm not the kind of guy that sits with committees, et cetera. I told you before, I'm a one-man committee. I mean, that's why I have the reputation I have, and that's why Dr. D came to me, and that's why the Board appreciated me, not because I'm going to show up at committees. I start work 5:00 in the morning, I work until late at night. I ain't going to Development Committee meetings.... So you can't get to this nitty gritty. It's ridiculous. Come on. How about this, how about that. Come on. I don't even have time to read this stuff. (Testimony, pp. 2495-96)

A: The idea that this is a cranky right-wing group is crazy. It's really crazy. I mean, you're talking to a left wing liberal. I'm as close to a communist as you can get and still be in business.... You know, I see—kids come to me all the time. I see more kids than you see, you know, and I cry for them. They're college graduates and they don't know nothing. It's the age of information, and they don't know nothing.... (Testimony, p. 2503)

Further, given the background, interests, and abilities of the majority of college students and how ill-prepared they would be for an academically rigorous course of study—especially those that Adelphi University might attract—the direction being set by the administration had very little chance of succeeding. It is perilous to assume that more than a handful of undergraduates are as interested in diligent study and learning as they are in high grades, certification, the social aspects of college life, and, in the end, a job. Even President Diamandopoulos in 1997 publicly acknowledged this truth: "Our nation carries an historical antipathy to the imperatives of serious education—we have no particular love of knowledge that is not immediately practical, and we resent being told what to do and that we ought to do it better."[26] It is unfortunate that he failed to come to this understanding until after the bloodletting—much of which was the result of his lapses in common sense and decency—at Adelphi.

Moreover, the precarious financial condition of the great majority of institutions of higher learning—again, especially Adelphi—and the invariable reluctance of faculty to embrace changes that might threaten their security and way of doing things were additional factors likely to jeopardize Diamandopoulos's majestic plans, no matter in theory how invaluable, well meaning, and educationally sound. President Diamandopoulos convinced the Board of Trustees otherwise. In addition, it never questioned his assertions that those who found fault with his dreams were not only obstructionists, but were intellectually and morally greatly inferior to him and his allies.

"The Greek Connection, so to Speak"

President Diamandopoulos never attempted to hide how attached he was to all things Greek. He scheduled a Board of Trustees meeting in Athens "to induce [the members] to look at the Parthenon, to think about the connection between democracy and education, to review the history of the West, to explore the possibility that Greek leaders might be persuaded to help us with wealth."[27] He arranged for Adelphi to host a national Greek soccer team, at a time when the school's athletic

scholarships were being cut. This cost $250,000 in campus improve-
ments that included a new press box, signs in Greek, a grandstand,
state-of the-art goals, and an additional public address system.

Between 1991 and 1995, Adelphi University awarded over 10 per-
cent of its honorary degrees to individuals with distinctly Greek names:
Ilias Lalaounis, Doctor of Fine Arts; Speros Vryonis, Jr., Doctor of
Humane Letters; George N. Hatsopoulos, Doctor of Science; Stavros
Xarhakos, Doctor of Fine Arts; and Dimitris L. Avramopoulos, Doc-
tor of Laws.

During his tenure, Diamandopolous was also able to recruit to the
1996 Adelphi Board four individuals who shared his Greek ancestry
—Dimitri Contominas, Peter Goulandris, Elias Kulukundis, and Nicholas P. Samios. (George C. Andreas and Bob K. Bakalis were also
persuaded by President Diamandopoulos to join the Board, but had
left it by 1996.) Obviously, not everyone of the same extraction shares
the same views on education or, for that matter, even more deeply
held views on, for example, religion, but at least as far as the former is
concerned, these individuals—the President referred to these Trustees
as "the Greek connection, so to speak"—did.

It is hard not to believe that common Greek descent was one element that contributed to the unshakable delusion of at least some
Trustees that the administration of Adelphi was in competent and
trustworthy hands. The testimony bears out the supposition that the
President was instrumental in having a Greek contingent—"people
who had money who were of Greek origin or from Greece"—added to
the Board.

Peter Goulandris:

A: I joined the Board in June of 1992, if I'm not mistaken.

Q: And prior to joining the Board did you have connection with Adelphi
University, sir?

A: None whatsoever.

Q: Prior to joining the Board, did you know Peter Diamandopoulos?

A: Yes, I had met Peter on several occasions.

Q: Of a social nature, Mr. Goulandris?

A: Of a social nature.

Q: And was it Mr. Diamandopoulos who recruited you to join the Board of Trustees of Adelphi University?

A: Well, Mr. Diamandopoulos certainly interested me in the University. He invited me to meet several of the other Trustees. And I attended a very pleasant luncheon at the Union League Club .... (Testimony, pp. 2311-12)

Whatever contributions to Adelphi resulted from Diamandopoulos's forays into Greece and his overtures to Greek-Americans, we can see by the paltry increases in the School's endowment that they were for the most part—with a few notable exceptions—modest.

In fact, the Committee to Save Adelphi denounced "the Greek connection, so to speak," indicating that some of its members' involvement in illegal activities could have grave implications for Adelphi:

> In 1989, the National Bank of Greece was fined by the federal government for money laundering, in which Atlantic Bank, a subsidiary of the National Bank of Greece, served as an intermediary. We believe that Peter Diamandopoulos was a member of Atlantic Bank's board of directors during that time. We know that he resigned from the board in 1991. Peter John Goulandris, current vice-chair of the Adelphi Board and next in line for its chairmanship, also sat on the board of Atlantic Bank. He resigned from the Atlantic Bank board in 1994. We have information that Diamandopoulos was paid while serving on the Atlantic board. Considering the charges against the bank, the relationship seems inappropriate at the least, and may, at its worst, hide serious criminal activity. (Exhibit, P-326)

This matter was not pursued by the Board of Regents in its inquiry.

The close relationship between governing boards and academic administrators works to the disadvantage of faculty, and, more generally, of many colleges and universities. The drawbacks for the institution of lay governing boards are amplified by how members are identified and selected.[28] The greater the imbalance of power on a campus, the greater the probability of its abuse. More on this in chapter 3.

Notes

1. New York: King's Crown Press.
2. The New York State law giving the Board of Regents the power to intervene in the conflict at Adelphi and remove its Board of Trustees is the only one of its

kind in the United States. The law is intended to give colleges and universities an opportunity to continue with new leadership rather than face closure. Other states rely on a more severe measure: revocation of an institution's charter, although it is unclear whether this has ever been done. Colleges and universities usually fail on their own. In Massachusetts in 1993, the attorney general investigated the charge that Boston University had awarded contracts to companies in which trustees had financial interests. There were no criminal charges, but the president, Adelphi Trustee John Silber, did return a bonus of $386,700 he had received from the board in 1989 for the role he played in selling a university-owned biotechnology company.

The New York law was enacted after World War 1, and prior to the Adelphi case, the Board of Regents rarely invoked it, dismissing trustees only three other times. In 1921, it removed the trustees of New York Medical College and Hospital for Women after it had suffered a number of financial setbacks and alumni asked for new management. In 1979, in the wake of incessant conflict and turmoil surrounding the dismissal of two dozen faculty and shrinking enrollments, most of the trustees of Mannes College of Music were replaced. It turned out the college was actually in debt. In a case in some ways similar to that of Adelphi, the trustees of the Chiropractic College of New York were removed in 1986. The principal charge was that some had used their position on the board to enrich their business interests.

3. Ibid. p.148.
4. Ibid. p.117.
5. Ibid. p. 148.
6. The initial letter to the State Education Department, November 20, 1995, suggested three general failures of the Board of Trustees: "We believe that actions by the Board of Trustees of Adelphi and its senior officers demonstrate a breach of fiduciary responsibilities, damaging lack of oversight, and excessive enrichment at the expense of the health and mission of the University." The attached five-page petition spelled out the specifics, some proven, some erroneous, and some irrelevant. There were four broad categories of charges.
"I. NON ARMS-LENGTH BUSINESS TRANSACTIONS WITH BOARD OF TRUSTEES"
A number of instances of "serious conflicts of interest" were mentioned in this section. It was alleged that the law firm of one Trustee "received significant legal fees from the University;" that the advertising agency of one Trustee "in handling ad campaigns for the University...stands to reap significant commissions;" that the company owned by one Trustee profited greatly from managing the University's insurance business; that the wife of one Trustee drawing a large salary from the University "was not regularly on campus to work;" that the telephone company of which one Trustee was an executive was awarded a $2 million contract by the University; that the construction company owned by one Trustee "has reportedly done a large amount of business with the University;" that there was "extensive bid-rigging activity" in awarding University contracts "to give business to interested or related parties." The question was also asked why after being "indicted for bank fraud, bribery, mail and wire fraud in federal court," one Trustee would "still be permitted to serve on our Board."
"II. BOARD MEETINGS AND OTHER TRIPS TO GREECE"
This charge refers to trips to Greece by the President, other administrators, spouses, and Trustees "allegedly under the guise of fundraising and recruitment" and other University business; they were not "legitimate," and they "represent excessive

expenditures with minimal benefit, at a time of fiscal constraint in the rest of the University."

"III. BENEFITS CONFERRED UPON PETER DIAMANDOPOULOS"

The accusation is made that the Board "has been lavish in the level of salary, benefits, and perks accorded" to President Diamandopoulos. The Committee cites his reputed 1993-94 compensation of $523,636, a condominium purchased in Manhattan by the University for $1.17 million for his use, other property purchased in Garden City under-utilized or provided rent-free to other administrators, an almost unlimited expense account for the President and one other administrator, high-priced automobiles and a chauffeur at the President's disposal, the luxurious renovations and furnishing of administrative offices, and the acquisition of art, furniture, and books for the President's personal use. The Committee contends that such expenditures are "impossible to justify given our current enrollment, fundraising, and financial situation."

"IV. FAILURES OF MANAGEMENT"

In addition to reiterating previous charges, the Committee also cites declining enrollments, Adelphi's faltering reputation, and excessive administrative turnover as clear indications of incompetent administration. As far as the Committee was concerned, that the Board of Trustees could not or would not look into this obvious epidemic of problems, and continued in its unwavering support of President Diamandopoulos, "represent[s] a breach of financial responsibility and a damaging lack of oversight," requiring "assistance" by the Board of Regents.

　　Although marked by many misstatements—for example, the contract awarded to the telephone company was for $1.25 million, not $2 million—the letter set out the parameters of the case against the Adelphi Board.

7.　Francis Wayland, *Thoughts on the Present Collegiate System in the United States,* Boston: Gould, Kendall, & Lincoln, 1842, p. 52.

8.　Ibid. p. 51.

9.　Edward C. Elliott, M. M. Chambers, and William A. Ashbrook, *The Government of Higher Education: Designed for the Use of University and College Trustees,* New York: American Book Company, 1935, pp. 50-51.

10.　Max McConn, *College or Kindergarten?,* New York: New Republic, Inc., 1928, p. 257.

11.　This is not at all unusual or surprising. In answer to the question: "Why is it essential that the president of the institution be present at board meetings?", Elliott, Chambers, and Ashbrook recommend: "Because the board is in practically constant need of information regarding the institution which the president is in a position to supply with minimum effort and delay. Furthermore, because of his intimate knowledge of the institution and its needs, he is normally expected to initiate most of the measures which receive the board's attention." Op. cit., p. 188. What is noteworthy here is the vigorous denial at Adelphi (and other institutions of higher learning) that this is, indeed, the case.

12.　John E. Kirkpatrick, *Force and Freedom in Education,* Yellow Springs, OH: The Antioch Press, 1929, p. 56.

13.　Richard Hofstadter, *Academic Freedom in the Age of the College,* New York: Columbia University Press, 1961, p. 120. An even harsher assessment of the negative effects on faculty is found in an early American Association of University Professors study of their marginal role in academic governance:

　　The actual teachers themselves have little or no legally recognized voice in the determination of the conditions, in the matters of fundamental university policies, academic status and salaries, under which they work. It is argued that this situation is responsible, in part, for the timidity and lack of enterprise and spirit of so many university teachers; that they tend to become either creatures of trivial pedagogical routine, deficient in the spirit of personal independence and intellectual creativeness, or discontented rebels, because they are parts of a system in the guidance and reform of which they do not effectively participate. It is argued that men qualified for intellectual leadership will not enter an occupation in which they cannot be intellectual stimulators and originators and gain decent livelihoods thereat. Critics further say that the type of organization at present prevailing seems designed for quantity production in credits and degrees, and that the result is that we have too large a proportion of mediocre and mechanized teachers engaged in turning out ever increasing numbers of graduates without any clear sense of, or respect for, the nature and value of scholarship and thoughtfulness. They attribute this situation to the autocratic type of university organization.

(J. A. Leighton (Chairman), "Report of Committee T on Place and Function of Faculties in University Government and Administration," *Bulletin of the American Association of University Professors,* Volume 6, Number 1, January 1920, pp. 21-22).

14. See Theresa Agovino, "A Modern-Day Socrates: Adelphi's Head Plots New Course," *Crain's New York Business,* 18 March, 1991, pp. F3 and 26.
15. Upton Sinclair, *The Goose-Step: A Study of American Education,* Pasadena, California: published by the author, 1922, p. 388.
16. Warren Bennis, *The Leaning Ivory Tower,* San Francisco, CA: Jossey-Bass, 1973, p. 16.
17. *The Centennial at Adelphi: One Hundred Years of American Higher Education,* pp. 12-13.
18. Ibid., pp. 10-16.
19. As an editorial note, it should be mentioned that this is not an attempt in any way to demean or belittle this position here as it is a view which I share.
20. I. M. Rubinow, "The Revolt of a Middle-Aged Father," *Atlantic Monthly,* Volume 139, Number 5, May 1927, p. 599.
21. See Alan Charles Kors and Harvey A. Silverglate, *The Shadow University: The Betrayal of Liberty on America's Campuses,* New York: The Free Press, 1998. Contrary to what too many believe, not everyone concerned with reports of faculty openly pushing what presently goes for a liberal agenda in the classroom is a troglodyte. Silverglate, for example, is a prominent civil libertarian. President Diamandopoulos, however was clearly sympathetic to causes and people well right of center. During his presidency, Adelphi University made contributions to, among others, Republican Governor George Pataki and the Foundation for Cultural Review, and awarded a disproportional number of honorary degrees to champions of conservative and reactionary ideas (e.g., Edward Teller, Gertrude Himmelfarb, Robert H. Bork, Richard Pipes, Paul Johnson, William F. Buckley, Jr., and Norman Podhoretz) and those employed by a Republican White House (e.g., Leonard Garment, Richard Cheney, and Peggy Noonan).
22. William Simon, "Paying a Price for Campus P.C.," *Washington Times,* 10 September, 1995, (Part B, Commentary), p. B1.
23. Maurice Cowling, "Peterhouse on Long Island," *Spectator,* Volume 278, 22 March, 1997, p. 24.
24. James Engell and Anthony Dangerfield, "The Market-Model University: Humanities in the Age of Money," *Harvard Magazine,* Volume 100, Number 5, May/June 1998, p. 50.

25. Mark Edmundson, "On the Uses of a Liberal Education: I. As Lite Entertainment for Bored College Students," *Harper's Magazine,* Volume 295, Number 1768, September 1997, p. 44.
26. Peter Diamandopoulos, "Lots of Luck to Clinton on Schools," *Newsday,* 11 February 1997, p. A27.
27. Doreen Carajal, "President's Pay[Compensation] Rankles Some at Adelphi," *New York Times,* 30 September 1995, p. 26. On October 26, 1995, attorneys for Adelphi sent a brief explanation of the Board meeting in Greece to the office of the New York State attorney general:

> The Board meeting was held in Athens with the purpose of connecting symbolically the mission of the University and the history of education back to Athens as the Board considered launching a greatly needed fund-raising campaign. The meeting was co-sponsored by two Trustees—President Peter Diamandopoulos and Trustee Contominas.

> The costs associated with the meeting were covered as follows: 1) Travel—each Trustee paid for their [sic] own arrangements; the University paid for three senior staff members and for the President; 2) Entertainment, food, receptions—Trustee Contominas paid for all food, entertainment, and a reception for top Greek leadership including distinguished educational, political, and cultural leaders to meet the Trustees, and to hear the mission of the University presented by the President. The purpose of the reception was cultivation for fund-raising and recruitment; 3) Lodging—President Diamandopoulos personally paid for the lodging of all Trustees during the meeting of the Board in Athens.

Less than two weeks later (November 6) the Committee to Save Adelphi sent a memorandum to the same office which raised questions about this account.

> We believe that the University may have paid for Igor Webb's wife to travel to the Board meeting in Greece, in violation of the University's own regulations. Evidence of this comes from Suzanne Sykes, former purchasing manager.

> Diamandopoulos has made inconsistent statements regarding how this trip was financed. He stated at a faculty meeting in September, 1994 that he had personally paid for the entire trip. He told the *New York Times* reporter that two Board members paid for the trip. Now he is claiming that the cost of the trip was shared by himself, Board members, and that the University paid for senior staff members....

28. It is widely believed that in recent years achievement has become more central in an appointment to a board, while the importance of ascription has decreased. There is little evidence to support this conviction. It is an open question whether much has changed since the fictional George Apley wrote the following to his son in 1933:

> Here, by the way, is something I wish to advance to you confidentially. I have heard from very good authority that there may be a vacancy in the Harvard Corporation. Certain of us are looking for a younger man and one of the right sort. There is altogether too much sentiment here lately for getting outsiders and so-called "new blood" into Harvard. The tradition of the place must not be

spoiled. There is actually some talk about a new president, about whom no one seems to have heard. Needless to say, this is only one of the wild rumours which circulate at such a time. Harvard will be Harvard, just as Harvard was old when Yale was but a pup. Seriously, I think you might be fitted to take your place on the corporation. It is true you have never been a scholar but now that you are actually going to live in Boston this does not really make much difference. I shall have some of the right people meet you and we shall see what can be done.(John P. Marquand, *The Late George Apley: A Novel in the Form of a Memoir,* New York: Random House, 1940. pp. 352-53).

3

The President and His Board II:
Mutual and Unqualified Faith

It is not difficult to understand why members of the Board of Trustees of Adelphi University were convinced of the great accomplishments of President Diamandopoulos and of the malfeasance of the
faculty. Board meetings were generally held in Manhattan, and most
Trustees rarely visited the campus. In addition, after approval of a
University policy in 1995 that the faculty could not initiate contact
with Trustees, essentially all that Board members knew about the
faculty was what they were told by the President and his circle. He
had a high opinion of himself and a low opinion of most faculty—
especially those most opposed to his policies—and he was not reluctant to convey this to the Board. The contempt in which most Board
members held faculty was staggering, and would likely make many
academics across the country wince. The Board's unquestioning loyalty and will to believe was firm. One after another, members of the
Board expressed their convictions about Diamandopoulos's extraordinary abilities and the faculty's extraordinary inadequacy or unruliness.
The hyperbole is breathtaking.

John Silber:

A: That he had created a highly intelligent, convincing, indeed compelling,
understanding of the way in which the general educational principles of science, mathematics, history, philosophy, sociology and the social sciences relate
to the professional programs, and how they all had to be in an intellectual
suspension as a part of the identity of Adelphi. (Testimony, p. 1545)

Q: Did you require that he report at the end of his sabbatical to the University?

A: ...It would be no more required for him than to require Einstein to find out whether he was going to file a report. When you achieve a certain level of excellence and a certain level of consistent performance, you don't have to treat somebody as if he's Johnny in the first grade. (Testimony, p. 1606)

A: Well, he's discussed it [resigning] with me off and on, because there have been problems with an incredibly ungrateful faculty ever since he's there, a resentful faculty, and consequently, having devoted himself as hard as he has to decreasing their teaching load, to increasing their salaries, to try to contribute to their welfare by the renovation of their offices and their classrooms, the ingratitude that he has felt has been something that has troubled him and it has caused him continually—not continually, but from time to time to ask, you know, is it worthwhile to continue to put out the way he has, which is 70, 80, a hundred hours a week. (Testimony, pp. 1611-12)

Peter Goulandris:

A: And the other [reason for the concern that the President could leave the University] relates to Dr. Diamandopoulos's brilliance and the demand for his services elsewhere....

A: But there had certainly been a history, as high as our regard is for our faculty and as hard as we've tried to improve their circumstances and help them be better teachers and have better lives, we have not always gotten the same manner of cooperation from the union. I think that's very regrettable. And, in fact, I'm not sure why I see it's necessary....

A: Well, I consider that Dr. Diamandopoulos is one of the top educators in the country....

Q: Is there anything else that you used to make your assessment that Dr. Diamandopoulos is one of the leading educators in the United States and abroad?

A: I have to use my best judgment on that, ma'am; I think I did. (Testimony, pp. 2339-42)

George Lois:

A: I've never seen anything like the guy. Twenty-four hours a day, that's all he thinks about, the school. He's unhappy with everything that happens because he wants perfection.... I mean, he's a good guy. He's the good guy. I admire him greatly.... But you know what I recognized in him? I recognized in him—I think I recognized in him incredible intellect, incredible passion and humanity, and incredible leadership, and I can't give up [on] a guy like that. (Testimony, pp. 2427-29)

A: Before Dr. "D" took over, it was a dog university. D-o-g, dog. He took it over, and he took over a school that was going out of business, and he saved the University. He's trying to build a great school, and he's one of the great men in American education.... (Testimony, p. 2461)

A: The guy has a vision, and that's the—he's building the school one mentor at a time. Isn't that terrible? God, don't you think everybody in America should be doing what Dr. "D" does? My God. If everyone was as good as Dr. "D" this would be a great world. (Testimony, p. 2501)

A: A lot of them [the faculty] [are] lazy, didn't work that hard, maybe weren't great teachers. I mean, there was dissatisfaction, that we have to continually improve the faculty. (Testimony, pp. 2531-32)

It is somewhat unnerving to think of the potential damage one individual—a well educated man, a philosopher by training—could inflict on an institution and its faculty, not only by his actions but by his words. However, the focus here should not be on the antics of President Diamandopoulos. What occurred illustrates the danger inherent in the uneven distribution of power in American institutions of higher learning. One or a few individuals can wreak havoc, maybe not on an entire campus, but certainly on the personal lives of unprotected faculty. The tradition of co-option greatly increases the possibility of this happening.

Assuring Consensus

Given that individuals feel most comfortable with others who hold similar world views and values and that groups will recruit others most like themselves,[1] it is still remarkable how intolerant Adelphi Trustees were of those who did not see things exactly as they did. This was true not only for dissenting faculty, but even for colleagues. Those with misgivings about any decision taken by the leadership of the Trustees were summarily denied a hearing, fair or unfair. They were dismissed out of hand as troublemakers. What they said and did was discredited. They were looked upon and treated as enemies. There was an obsession on the part of many on the Board for keeping its deliberations and decisions secret. The case of Trustee William Borten is instructive here, showing that there were risks even for members of the Board who might not be true believers and might at some point break ranks.

Becoming an Outsider: One Example

Borten's estrangement from his fellow Trustees began in 1990 when he was chairman of the Board's Finance Committee. After a comprehensive review of the University's financial records, he concluded that spending $7,500 a month to rent an apartment in Manhattan for President Diamandopoulos was an inappropriate use of University funds. This view was not shared by the majority of the Trustees, and the apartment was leased. A successful business executive, Borten was not easily deterred, and he continued to ask questions about University expenditures.

Borten focused primarily on the disproportionate growth in administrative salaries compared with teaching salaries. His more general concern was about the growth of administrative costs at the University. He discovered that between 1987-88 and 1990-91, at a time when enrollment was at best flat, there was a 57 percent increase in administrative salaries and a 6 percent increase in faculty salaries. By his calculations, the number of faculty had increased by two, while the support staff had increased by thirty-seven, from 295 to 332. The budget for the latter increased from $8.8 million to $11.4 million, or nearly 30 percent.

Borten asked for more detailed information from the administration. After a number of exchanges of letters, evasions, and considerable delay, all that he was given were summary figures of compensation for full-time employees broken down into broad categories: faculty, buildings and grounds, employees not covered by contractual agreements, deans, directors, and so forth. There were salary ranges, maximums, minimums, and averages for various categories. The data were sketchy, but what he found was disturbing. For example, with a net increase of one position, the salaries for the category of directors had increased $400,000. (Board chair Byrne's wife was at that time the director of alumni relations.)

Borten persisted in his efforts to obtain a list of job titles and the salary for each. On November 24, 1990, he wrote to President

Diamandopoulos requesting "a more comprehensive explanation" to his "questions related particularly to the growth of support staff wage and salary expenditures from 1987-88 to 1990-91." In concluding he insisted, "I would like to have answers to these questions on or before the date set for the next meeting of the Finance Committee, December 5, 1990." President Diamandopoulos responded five days later:

> Since the information you ask [for] in this letter, I believe, has already been sent to you in copious form; and since I don't understand what else you are really searching for or demand to know—about policy, practice, records, etc.— I am sending you no new material until the nature and appropriateness of your request is discussed before the Board at its next meeting.

> Incidentally, trustees of university boards normally communicate with their presidents in collegial and informal terms. And never in a peremptory style.

(The brusqueness of President Diamandopoulos's reply may offer a clue about the actual relative power of a governing board member and an academic administrator, at least at Adelphi in 1990.)

Borten described both the next committee meeting and Board meeting as "being tense." At a reception that evening, "I called Jim Byrne, who was then chairman [of the Board], aside, and I said, 'Jim, I'm not happy about the fact that I'm not getting this data. I want to know specifics of what people are being paid.'... [A]nd his comment was, 'I don't think you need it.' I said, 'Well, I do think I need it, and if you're unwilling to provide it, I don't think I can continue to serve on this Board of Trustees.' And I remember it was very tense" (Testimony, pp. 52-54).

The following week, Borten received a letter from Byrne dropping him from the Board:

> I have had several days to reflect on our conversation following last Wednesday's Board of Trustees meeting. After serious consideration, I have unfortunately come to the conclusion that you and I have an irreconcilable deep philosophical difference concerning the discharge of the responsibilities of a Trustee as well as my role and obligations as the duly elected chair of the Board. This assessment of the situation is shared by all of the officers of the Board as well as other key Trustees.

> Regrettably, I have decided to accept your resignation as a member of the Board of Trustees of Adelphi University effective immediately as tendered to me at last Wednesday's Board meeting.

> You have my best wishes for your future endeavors.

William Borten:

Q: Again, in your view, before December 10th, had you actually tendered your resignation?

A: No, I quite specifically said, "Jim, I'm going to have to think about this if you can't provide the data." (Testimony, pp. 64-65)

With the use of such methods to promote consensus, it was not difficult for President Diamandopoulos and the Board he surrounded himself with to achieve it. Trustees who were not team players were unwelcome.

Trustee Nadel: A Second Example

Leonard Nadel, who had been chair of the Board and chair of the search committee that selected Diamandopoulos as President, divulged in an interview with the *LI Business News* ("Nadel Blasts Adelphi's President," 31 July, 1989) that Diamandopoulos even engineered his unwanted retirement.

LIBNews: What are your feelings about the current situation at Adelphi University...?

Nadel: It was a sad day indeed for Adelphi when Dr. Diamandopoulos became its President....

LIBNews: Briefly describe your relationship with Adelphi and your responsibilities there.

Nadel: Until I left the Board, I was affiliated with Adelphi for about 25 years. I began there as a member of the advisory board of the School of Social Work. After serving on the board of the School of Social Work, I then became chair of that board for 11 years, roughly half of which time, I was also on the University Board. I am not an alumni of Adelphi, actually I am a graduate of NYU but I received an honorary doctorate from Adelphi after I had completed six years as chairman of the Board of Trustees....

LIBNEWS: Can you tell us about the events that led up to your choosing Dr. Peter Diamandopoulos as President of the University?

Nadel: One of my assignments—actually my last assignment of any major consequence on the Board of Trustees—was to be chairman of the presidential search committee. I had served on a previous presidential search committee,

though not as its chairman, when we selected Tim Costello some years back....
We worked long and hard to find an appropriate individual to become President....

Though we recognized that Diamandopoulos was going to be far stronger in
his dealing than his predecessors because of his personality, we were not
looking for someone who was going to be a martinet.

LIBNews: Had you been aware of the constant conflict with the faculty during
his previous six-year term as President of Sonoma State University in California?

Nadel: We knew there was a problem out there. The manner in which it was
explained to us by both him and others made it sound far less damaging to him
and his reputation than now seems to be coming out of the woodwork.

LIBNews: Do you feel the search committee was misled?

Nadel: Our presidential search committee was deluded into thinking we had
found someone who would prove to be not only a noteworthy academician but
an experienced and sensitive administrator. He is a noteworthy academician,
though he has no regard for the professional schools that did so much to build
the University's reputation over the years. Also he has proven to be totally
lacking in the administrative skills so essential to a well managed institution.
He lacks the human relations ingredient so important to any chief executive,
whether it be in a business corporation or at a university, where many of the
elements found in any business enterprise also exist....

LIBNews: Why did you leave your position at Adelphi?

Nadel: I was pushed out by the President. I'm sure you have many of the facts
which describe incident after incident of mishandling by the University management. The turnover at all levels has been horrendous, to his detriment....
Even the Board of Trustees has been decimated over the past few years. Those
who are on the Board today are his personal choices, all beholden to him.
Trustees who gave many years of devoted service to Adelphi, many who are
illustrious alumni, have either been pushed off the Board by his design or have
left on their own volition after becoming totally disenchanted with what they
saw happening. Even Randall McIntyre and myself who were Board chairmen
collectively for eleven years were released without explanation because we
found the role of yes men to his every whim abhorrent and out of character
with the kind of responsible leadership of days gone by. The Board meets with
much less frequency, subject to his agenda, and to rubber stamping his programs and plans as it has been reported to me.

If we go through that search committee, just four years later, the only one that I
can recall still remaining at Adelphi is Jim Byrne, the current chairman of the
Board of Trustees.

LIBNews: Do you feel Byrne is acting properly as chairman of the Board of Trustees?

Nadel: Jim Byrne appears to be under the sway of the President. This is also a personal hurt to me because I feel responsible for bringing Jim Byrne along. He was an assistant chairman of the Board under me, as was Dick Lovely. His career was sponsored by me in a number of situations.... Only to find that he has been a major disappointment. He doesn't want to talk to anybody because he is in a very delicate and difficult situation.... Faculty and administrative appointments have been made arbitrarily, without proper search procedures— all of these actions flaunt the required procedures and are further evidence of the heavy-handed and dictatorial methods currently employed at Adelphi....

LIBNews: Do you blame yourself for Dr. Diamandopoulos's appointment?

Nadel: This is a dangerous man who functions as a despot in a totalitarian state. He has in a few years managed to antagonize the students and faculty to a point of seeking his removal—no mean accomplishment for such groups of independent thinkers and academic spirits.... A fine institution has fallen into the hands of a scheming and self-serving tyrant for which all of us must accept our share of the blame. As the chairman of the presidential search committee who recommended him to the Board of Trustees, I must admit it is the single worst example of poor judgment that a number of us exercised in our professional careers, one that I will always regret.

What stands out from this exchange, even more than Nadel's disenchantment with President Diamandopoulos, is the manifestly poor judgment on the part of the Trustees in selecting Diamandopoulos as President in the first place. The Adelphi Board is not the only lay board, presently or in the past, incapable of evaluating the capacity of an academic administrator, someone upon whom it is bestowing considerable responsibility and power. This point is considered in greater depth in chapter 5.

Despite Nadel's contention, Diamandopoulos was not "a noteworthy academician," not even a noteworthy academic. The Board, Nadel claimed, was also seeking an "experienced" administrator. Diamandopoulos was surely experienced, but this experience had shown him to be an unqualified failure (again, more of this in chapter 5). For boards to turn to academic administrators for recommendations or assessments to assist them in the selection of a college or university executive in the belief that they are receiving qualified advice, is hardly a solution to the dilemma lay boards face. After all, other academic administrators have been chosen in this same haphazard way. Given these circumstances, it is testimony to the validity of Cohen and March's conclusion that what academic administrators do "will not matter much" and to the strength of institutions of higher learning to muddle through, that they continue to function in light of the imperfections in their methods of choosing those charged with managing them.

Although sometimes lacking in specifics, Nadel's explosive public revelations did nothing to change the situation at Adelphi; they did little more than bring a few letters to the editor, both complimenting and condemning Nadel. John Silber's response on August 21, 1989 was perhaps the most strident:

> Never have I read such an extraordinary and indiscreet piece of self-serving balderdash. Apparently, former chairman Leonard Nadel has forgotten the condition to which Adelphi University sank under his chairmanship. Had it not been for the appointment of a vigorous, highly qualified, idealistic, and courageous President, Adelphi might well be bankrupt and in receivership today. When the Board at Adelphi appointed Diamandopoulos, they knew they were bringing a controversial leader to the campus. They did so because they knew that they had to have a leader who would make the painful changes that were necessary in order for Adelphi to survive. It is regretable [sic] that Nadel, who had the insight to recognize the need for change, could not accommodate himself to the changes that he knew were necessary. It is bad enough that he should attack Diamandopoulos; it is shameful that he should attack Jim Byrne, his successor to the chairmanship of the Board of Trustees. It is very sad when players in life do not know how to gracefully leave the stage. Bitterness makes a sorry exit....

Borten and Nadel were not the only Trustees prodded to leave the Board, unhappy with its decisions on a number of issues. After Trustee Robert McMillan suggested on television that the Board should consider meeting with faculty to hear their grievances, he was publicly rebuked by Trustee Joseph Carlino, and soon resigned. At about the same time, Thomas Lovely, a prominent Adelphi graduate who for many years had served as vice chair of the Board, fell out of favor and soon departed. (Two former Trustees [Rico and Biddell] who had left the Board prior to 1985 joined the petitioners in the action before the Board of Regents.)

Byrne testified that he was pivotal to a plan to change the membership of the Board in the late 1980s.

James T. Byrne, Jr.:

Q: And Mr. McIntyre, sir, how long had he been on the Board of Trustees?

A: Probably for an equal length of time.

Q: And he was encouraged to take emeritus status, sir?

A: That's correct.

Q: Let's see if you can help me with some other names of people who left the Board of Trustees during this period of time. Mr. Colasante, sir?

A: Scott Colasante, yes....

Q: How long had he been on the Board of Trustees, sir?

A: I think maybe three years....

Q: Was he a Trustee who had been suggested by the students, sir?

A: At some point in time, what we had done, the Board had created a position that would be filled by a recent graduate.....

Q: Who made the decision to discontinue this practice, sir?

A: I did....

Q: What was the rationale for discontinuing this practice?

A: The rationale for discontinuing the practice was the fact that the individuals who were—the last two individuals, and Mr. Colasante was one of them—holding those positions were having difficulty understanding that they did not represent a particular constituency,... and what was happening, for example, is that after every Board meeting, Mr. Colasante would call a meeting with the student body, and then give them chapter and verse on everything that was discussed at the Board meeting...

Q: What about George T. Conklin, if I'm saying his name correctly?

A: Mr. Conklin, I think, was on the Board for maybe 12 years or so....

Q: Now when you joined the Board of Trustees, was there a practice of having the chair of the Senate, that is, the Faculty Senate, attend at least part of the meetings of the Board of Trustees?

A: Yes, there was.

Q: Did the practice cease in the late 1980s, sir?

A: Yes, it did.

Q: Who made that decision, sir?

A: I did....

Q: What was the rationale for discontinuing the attendance of the representative of the Faculty Senate?

A: Well, it was a similar situation to what we had with the young Trustee in that the chair of the Senate would go back to the Senate and discuss with the

Senate in detail issues that were being discussed at the Board... nor did we want to invite individuals on a regular basis to the Board....

Q: Do you recall a representative of the Student Government Association coming to at least some meetings of the Board of Trustees?

A: Yes....

Q: Was there a decision made to discontinue that practice, sir?

A: Yes, there was.

Q: Who made that decision?

A: I did. (Testimony, pp. 5403-10)

The Board clearly had grave misgivings about dissenters; they were unceremoniously dropped. The view that the more secretive it was, the more it could accomplish, seemed pervasive. The Board rejected not only the presence of those who seemed to threaten the perceived need to conceal decisions, it isolated itself from them. The President assisted in these efforts; by the late 1980s, he had gone as far as to discontinue the practice of forwarding copies of the student newspaper to Board members.

In March 1989, a delegation of faculty asked to meet with the Board to air a number of grievances with regard to the University's administration. The Board denied the request, and reiterated its unequivocal support of President Diamandopoulos. In a letter, the chair of the Board explained why it "declines" to discuss faculty concerns:

> The Board has supported the President's strategy during the past three years to reduce dramatically the faculty's teaching load, provide significant salary increases, institute faculty merit awards, underwrite visits by distinguished outside faculty, and approve the appointment of forty-three new faculty. Clearly these actions, in endorsement of the President's recommendations and aims, indicate that the faculty are the first beneficiaries of Adelphi in a state of positive change. But there are reciprocal obligations in these developments.

> Therefore, it is the position of the Board that it is the professional and contractual obligation of the faculty, in cooperation with the President and his leadership team, to contribute to these essential and constructive steps, to achieve a stronger and better Adelphi.

> We know full well that President Diamandopoulos would welcome such cooperation.[2]

The faculty persisted; the specter of "a serious slowdown" was even raised by the chair of the Faculty Senate. He also warned that if the major matters of dispute were ignored, the result could be "the ultimate destruction of this University":

> The bottom line in this matter now boils down to human dignity and respect. As long as the Trustees act with such arrogance, some faculty members will risk destruction of the entire institution — just as many Eastern [Airlines] employees would sooner see the airline fold than work for people who treat them with contempt.

In all, the faculty made three approaches. The Board did not budge. Two Trustees summed up its view. Joseph F. Carlino: "President Diamandopoulos has our whole-hearted support. In light of that, we see no need to meet with the faculty and we have no intention of doing so." Hilton Kramer: "The Board already has made its position perfectly clear.... No other response is called for."[3]

By 1990, the Board was out of touch with a large part of the Adelphi community. Its understanding of campus life was filtered through President Diamandopoulos and his increasingly smaller circle. Attempts to penetrate the barriers the Board and the President had erected were unsuccessful. The Board, or its leadership, simply did not want information other than what it received from the administration.

James T. Byrne, Jr.:

Q: Has the chair of the Faculty Senate since then requested a discussion with the Board of Trustees?

A: I think on one occasion they had requested coming to the Board, and they did come to the Board.

Q: When was that, sir?

A: It was within several years after we discontinued the practice.

Q: Well, did the Faculty Senate ask to speak to the Board with respect to certain issues involving the Honors College, sir?

A: I know we had gotten a correspondence that they wanted to discuss the Honors College with us, yes.

Q: Did the Board make a determination to not have a discussion with the Faculty Senate, sir?

A: Yes, it did, because we had already approved the Honors College and it had already been approved by the faculty and the Faculty Senate. So we didn't see any need to have a discussion at that point. This was months after we approved it.

Q: Do you recall the one time when a member of the Faculty Senate did come to talk to the Board of Trustees?

A: No, I don't....

Q: Do you know if a security guard banned the head of the Faculty Senate in the late fall of 1988 from coming to the Board of Trustees meeting?

A: I have no idea what you're talking about. (Testimony, pp.5412-14)

Other Trustees with suggestions that might move the University in a direction to which Diamandopoulos and those closest to him were not committed were made to feel unwelcome, and in turn left the Board. Sheldon Weinig who was on the Board for three years wrote, "I must state categorically that it has not been a satisfying experience." At one point, Weinig suggested that an outside consultant Adelphi was about to hire "wasn't the right person." As he saw it, "my opinion was not only ignored, but I was emphatically told that I was completely wrong."

There were additional slights that Weinig suffered. After he was appointed to the Board's investment committee, he was sent a list of five possible meeting dates. He responded that there was only one which would preclude his attendance. The committee chose to meet at that time. He and his wife then decided to endow traveling fellowships for undergraduates. He reported that the effort was "trivialized and it was intimated that both the purpose and amount of money were inappropriate."[4]

Another Board member, an attorney, M. Curt Meltzer, had a similar experience in his attempt to foster an exchange program with Japan. He hoped to make an "approach to the Japanese community that I represent to obtain financial and possibly student exchange support from those sources." However, "no follow up by the dean or you was forthcoming." He also recommended that the extremely wealthy former Japanese ambassador to the United Nations and deputy secretary general of the OECD (Organisation for Economic Co-operation and Development), who in his own right was "a distinguished" scholar and author, be considered for University honors. His suggestion "was dismissed most arrogantly by Hilton Kramer [who labeled the diplomat] a 'petit bureaucrat.'" He was additionally annoyed that not only was his idea brushed aside, but that Adelphi chose to instead "honor that distinguished Greek scholar Telly Savalas." Meltzer subsequently resigned from the Board.[5]

Consequences I

When there are few or no significant limits to a president's influence on a governing board, or where a governing board has limited influence on a president, obvious consequences follow: presidents can do as they please, and there is no one to caution them when decisions are flawed.

A theme developed in the previous chapter was that one cannot even assume that a president and a board are independent. Normally, it is unusual for a board to appoint or delegate power to someone different in any significant way from its membership. That is why a college or university board and its administration can for the most part be seen as one and the same. In the case of Adelphi, a relatively long exchange between the chair of the Regents' subcommittee and an attorney for the Board of Trustees, showing how it became the handmaiden to the President, exemplifies this point.

> Q[from Regent]: Counsel has conferred and I want to direct a question myself on behalf of the panel to you, Mr. Shapiro, to Barry Shapiro of the Rivkin, Radler firm. What party or parties is your firm representing in this proceeding before the Regents' panel?
>
> A: We're representing the Trustees, as our papers indicate.
>
> Q: All of the Trustees?
>
> A: Yes, sir.
>
> Q: You're co-counsel with Mr. Conroy's firm?
>
> A: That's correct.
>
> Q: Have you represented the Trustees of Adelphi University in other matters?
>
> A: That's correct.

Q: How far back does that go, to the best of your recollection?

A: We represented the University in connection with the I.D.A. transaction, and we may have done some periodic work prior to that time for the University. I do not recall the specifics. It has not been on a regular basis since Richard Schure is the regular counsel to the University.

Q: Has your firm or you personally, Mr. Shapiro, ever represented Peter Diamandopoulos personally in his personal capacity?

A: In one or two instances.

Q: Would you tell us—without going into the attorney/client relationship, can you tell us what the subject matters were of those instances?

A: Just in the most general terms, we represented him in connection with a variety of sporadic personal matters relating to him as an individual.

Q: Did any of those personal matters relate to his compensation from Adelphi University?

A: No.

Q: And by compensation we're talking about the full compensation package including the letters of agreement we've read, the option to purchase the New York City condo?

A: We provided certain services in connection with those documents.

Q: Did your firm draft those documents, the documents of March 1994 that we've looked at?

A: Yes.

Q: Not just the condominium purchase agreement or contract of sale but also the letters we've been looking at too?

A: The letter of agreement and the separation agreement, that's correct.

Q: Right.

Q[another Regent]: So I'm clear about this, in Mr. Goulandris's letter when he says, "I've carefully reviewed each document of the package and after discussion approved it," the package refers to those documents which you drafted on behalf of Dr. Diamandopoulos and sent on to him?...

A: If that accompanied the documents that Regent Meyer just spoke to, then yes.

Q[first Regent]: When you prepared those documents, the letters we're talking about and the contract of purchase or contract of sale, in March 1994, did you believe that you or your firm were acting on behalf of the Trustees or on behalf of the President or both?

A: I believe we were preparing the documents for the President, really to facilitate the transaction. There was no negotiation that I participated in. President Diamandopoulos and I would discuss the documents and the documents were then drafted. So the capacity was mostly that of scrivener.

Q: Scrivener at whose direction?

A: I'm going to decline to answer that on the basis of attorney/client privilege. (Testimony, pp. 868-73)

There is little one could add to this stunning admission.

When the leadership of the board of a college or university and the president hold essentially identical views on how the institutions should function—at Adelphi the bond was cemented by a shared authoritarianism and disdain for faculty and others who questioned what they understood were their prerogatives—they can continue to work together whatever the criticisms or impediments for long periods of time.

What occurred at Adelphi was not an anomaly. It is best seen as an extreme example of how a determined and misguided board and administration, working together, can destabilize a college or university. Given the imbalance of power on American campuses, the probability of this occurring from time to time is moderately high. As Max Savelle wrote many years ago: "The fate of the university is in the hands of one man. All he [the president] has to do is convince the regents that they should support him; and if the regents are businessmen, with the 'businessman's concept' of the university, they usually will."[6] Savelle went on to observe:

In doing so [acting on the assumption that his personal judgment was more nearly infallible than that of the faculty], he [the president] has exposed the inherent weakness of the American university system: the separation of the ultimate power of decision from the community of scholars whose interests and whose work the decision most directly affects. The fault is not so much that of the individual president as it is of the system.[7]

Diamandopoulos may have overreached and the Adelphi Board of Trustees may have been too gullible and compliant, but there is no evidence that the broad picture described by Savelle has changed in the over four decades since it was written.

Consequences II

The relationship of the Board of Trustees to President Diamandopoulos at Adelphi obviously went well beyond simply being friendly and productive to one in which no glimmer of objectivity or independent judgment could be detected. The Board seemed to be mesmerized. Its primary allegiance was to Diamandopoulos rather than to the University. Accusations and adversity pushed the Board and the President even closer together. The attachment slowly evolved into a conspiracy.

To a number of the Trustees, Diamandopoulos was the embodiment of what higher education could do, and what Adelphi was on the threshold of becoming. They never doubted that he was a great man. Diamandopoulos was at the center in selecting most Board members, and this did a great deal to ensure that he would be esteemed and seen in this way. It was incomprehensible that others might hold a different view. Those who were challenging him were not simply wrong, they were incessant malcontents and troublemakers. At a Board meeting on December 6, 1995, the chair commented: "To our President, I commend you in behalf of our Board for your strength, courage, determination, composure in bearing the insults, falsehoods, and character assassination which we have endured together. The Judases responsible for this crucifixion will pay for their betrayal for Adelphi will rise quickly and become the great institution for which Peter Diamandopoulos has had visions of at the year 2000 and beyond." As incredible as it might seem, unfolding events and additional information did not weaken the Trustees' exalted regard for Diamandopoulos.[8]

Peter Goulandris:

Q: Do you agree with the statement by Chairwoman Procope?...

A: And I find them [the Committee to Save Adelphi and others] sadly misguided. I find them unfair, I find that it's a travesty; it's a negotiating tactic that's gone completely wild. I have never seen ad hominem attacks of the nature and of the virulence that some Board members and the President have had to sustain. I find it improper, and I would certainly back the sentiment of these. (Testimony, pp. 1683-85)

The effect of this solid alliance between the Board and President at Adelphi increased the imbalance of power; as most faculty saw it, it made their position nearly hopeless. The principles that appeared to be operating here were (1) the closer the relationship between a board and a school's president, the more that power will be concentrated; (2) the more that power is concentrated, the more potent it can be; (3) the more potent the power, the greater the imbalance in power between the faculty and the president/governing board; (4) and the greater the imbalance in power, the more disadvantaged faculty will become. All of this can readily be seen in actions the Adelphi Board of Trustees took in the first week of March 1994.

Two Sabbatical Policies

At its spring meeting, the Board, after hearing that a committee of their colleagues was "less than happy with the results of sabbatical reporting by the faculty," unanimously passed a resolution expressing "serious concern about the productivity of faculty on sabbatical" and requested that the administration establish "a data base that can provide an informed basis for future policies regarding sabbaticals." The Board wanted to evaluate "the utility of sabbaticals as a University investment...[so that at some future time they might] be enhanced, strengthened, or otherwise reconsidered." In brief, the Board had decided to reassess whether or not in the future it would continue to follow the policy of granting sabbatical leaves to faculty.[9] This decision takes on special significance when juxtaposed to one paragraph of a letter to President Diamandopoulos from the chair of the Board the following day regarding his terms of employment:

> Sabbatical. In view of your continued service to the University, as an active member of the faculty with classroom responsibilities, and in view of your heavily extended workday, workweek, and workyear as President of Adelphi, you shall be entitled to accrue sabbatical leave at the rate of one-sixth of a year's salary for every year of service commencing July 1, 1985. For example, after serving six years, you shall be entitled to a sabbatical of one full year at your rate of compensation at the time you take that leave. If you were to serve Adelphi for fourteen years, you would be entitled to two and one-third years of compensation at the rate in effect at that time. If you were to serve Adelphi for 18 years, you would be entitled to three full years of compensation at the rate in effect at that time. It is understood, moreover, that in the event of your death, your estate will receive the sabbatical compensation you have earned at the time of your death.

Diamandopoulos's good fortune will surely overwhelm those familiar with academic precedent or the academic reward structure. However, there is a larger point here. It is not so much that a governing board would agree to these arrangements, but that it had the incontrovertible right to do so. It could—particularly at a private institution of higher learning—do so with impunity. What else might governing boards do? A governing board can do just about as it wishes, and almost always out of public view, or, as it is generally put, in executive session. That most governing boards may not be as foolish or cavalier—they may or they may not be; there are too few records available to make an informed judgment—is really not the issue. To be sure, governing boards cannot break the law and get caught. This is at bottom what undid the Board of Trustees at Adelphi.

At Adelphi, there were no checks and balances. The Board and the President were one. Whatever decision Diamandopoulos might make, he could almost surely depend on the full support of the Board of Trustees. He was accountable to no one. All that he needed to do was to submit optimistic fiscal reports, act presidential, and continue to flatter the Trustees.

To bolster his position and ensure his dominance, Diamandopoulos directed the University's insurance business to Ernesta Procope, the chair of the Board of Trustees. Over a nine-year period, between 1987 and 1995, her firm, E.G. Bowman, received commissions of at least $1,227,949.[10]

Other individuals also profited from their membership on the Board. A considerable amount of the University's legal business was handled by a firm in which one Trustee was a partner. In 1995 and 1996, Adelphi's advertising account was given to Trustee George Lois's firm. By placing advertisements in the media, Lois received commissions of over $150,000. (The media insert invoices Lois's firm submitted to the University between September 28, 1995 and May 6, 1996 were for $869,501, and he received the standard commission, which is calculated at approximately 17.5 percent of this total.) Lois's company was also paid $214,138 by Adelphi University over a ten-month period for production expenses. About $36,000 of this went to Lois's son, principally for a series of photographs he took of some faculty between April and July 1995.

The wife of the previous chair of the Board, James T. Byrne, Jr., was rapidly promoted and given substantial salary increases during Diamandopoulos's presidency. In the fall after Diamandopoulos arrived at Adelphi, she was director of special events at an annual salary of $25,000. Three years later it was $50,000. The following year she was promoted to vice president for community relations and external affairs at a salary of $55,000. When she resigned that position four years later, her salary was $74,000.[11]

Through these strategems, Diamandopoulos acquired a number of unwavering patrons. There was no question that conflict of interest was of great interest those with power at Adelphi. The longer Diamandopoulos's tenure as President, the more some Board members were indebted to him, and the freer his hand in all matters, academic and otherwise. He soon came to understand that there was nothing he could not try, no matter how ill-advised.

No individual, regardless of how competent or lucky, can be successful all of the time. At some point, everyone stumbles. In the case of Diamandopoulos, his record at Adelphi shows more mistakes than that of the average academic administrator. However, his setbacks or failures never deterred him from moving on to his next injudicious scheme as these were never seen as setbacks or failures. The Board did not ask him to account for them. He praised the Board; it praised him.

Because Diamandopoulos accumulated relatively more power than most academic administrators, he was able to push ahead, scarcely heeding the consequences. He could use force and intimidation to get his way. Since the Board of Trustees was often misled by Diamandopoulos and knew little about academic matters, it was not difficult for him to conceal his poor judgment. He could blame mismanagement on others. Occasionally it was someone in his administration. Most of the time the miscreants were second-rate faculty that he had inherited—especially activists in the Faculty Senate or union whom he could not dismiss or dismiss only with great difficulty, because they were protected by continuing appointments (tenure). With regularity, he was rewarded irrespective of what he did or did not do.

During most of his time at Adelphi, Diamandopoulos ran the University as if it were his principality. He rewarded his allies with outsized academic salaries and other favors, even housing. He threatened and sometimes attempted to punish his opponents. Teaching assignments were often made that advantaged the former and disadvantaged the latter. There were abundant funds for the initiatives of allies; all others were lectured on the need for austerity.

The most favored individual at Adelphi was Diamandopoulos himself. He spent hundreds of thousands of dollars remodeling and decorating his office in marble, chrome, and leather. He was reimbursed a sum in excess of $360,000 for his travel and entertainment expenses between January 1993 through June 1996. (This amount does not include disbursements under $100 and a number of other expenditures paid directly by the University.) He felt free to make an illegal political contribution with University funds to Senator Gramm from Texas. When this was uncovered, it was attributed to faulty legal advice. That an academic administrator would find it necessary to seek the counsel of an attorney on a matter that was illegal and patently so unethical is itself telling. He charged the University for lavish Christmas checks he passed out to the doorman and other staff at his Manhattan apartment.

Countless examples could be added to this enumeration of Diamandopoulos's extravagances. However, this abbreviated list seems sufficient to show the effects of the imbalance of power in institutions of higher learning, the point being made.

The remarkable growth in Diamandopoulos's own compensation most clearly reflects his dominance at Adelphi:

1. His initial employment agreement in 1985 provided for an annual salary of $95,000, a TIAA-CREF (Teachers Insurance Annuity Association-College Retirement Equity Fund) contribution by the University of 13 percent of his salary, the use of the President's house free of cost, the use of an owned or leased University automobile, life insurance coverage in the amount of $500,000, reimbursement for domestic travel, "reasonable and necessary" expenses incurred in the performance of his duties, and stipends of approximately $5,000 and $12,000 to cover household help and expenses.
2. In 1986, his salary was increased to $145,000 and the University's TIAA-CREF contribution was increased to 15 percent of his salary.
3. In 1987, his salary rose to $175,000, his life insurance coverage was increased to $750,000, while the University's TIAA-CREF contribution was increased to 18 percent of his salary. A deferred compensation package, providing for annual contributions by Adelphi of $50,000 over ten years, was added.
4. In 1988, his salary was $187,000.
5. In 1989, his salary was $215,000.
6. In 1990, he did not receive a permanent salary increase, but instead was given a $25,000 bonus.
7. In 1991, his salary was increased to $250,000.
8. In 1992, he did not receive a permanent salary increase, but instead was given a $25,000 bonus.
9. In 1993, Diamandopoulos's salary had reached $300,000. His new contract called for an automatic annual increase of 5 percent thereafter, an

increase of the University's contribution to his deferred compensation package to 30 percent of his base salary, a retroactive right to the 1985 academic year to sabbatical leave at the rate of one-sixth of a year's salary for every year of service, and provided at University expense a $1 million valuable items insurance policy to cover his jewelry and art collection. Diamandopoulos was also given the right to purchase for $905,000 Adelphi's Manhattan apartment for which it paid $1,150,000 and on which he spent between $170,000 and $190,000 of University funds for renovations and furniture.

10. In 1994, his salary was increased to $315,000.
11. In 1995, his salary was increased to $330,750, as was his life insurance coverage to $1,250,000. (The University also agreed to reimburse him for income taxes he might be required to pay resulting from its payment of the premiums.)
12. In 1996, Diamandopoulos announced that he would forgo his automatic 5 percent increase, and his base salary remained at $330,750. He also waived the right to collect any compensation for taxes. In May 1996, he wrote that "in light of the continuing controversy and media distortions, I have decided to further defer the generous fringe benefits provided me in my latest contract—the gross-up of wages to compensate for the taxes I will owe on the various fringe benefits. I reserve the right to reinstate this provision, prospectively, in the future and will notify you, should I decide to do so."

According to calculations by the New York State Attorney General, including salary, fringe benefits, deferred compensation, and the University's costs associated with the maintenance and insurance of two residences and the Lincoln Town Car he used: "The total cost to the University of Diamandopoulos's compensation for the 1995-96 academic year amounted to approximately $837,000."[12]

If nothing else, Diamandopoulos was surely self-aggrandizing. If academic administrators had so little power and by the same token faculty had a fraction of the power attributed to them, these figures would be substantially smaller.[12]

It is now necessary to return to the general subject of lay governing boards, so as to better understand how what occurred at Adelphi could occur.

Notes

1. See "Pressures to Uniformity in Groups: Introduction," in Dorwin Cartwright and Alvin Zander, Editors, *Group Dynamics: Research and Theory* (third edition), New York: Harper & Row, 1968, pp. 139-51.
2. Letter from James T. Byrne, Jr. to Ronald S. Feingold, Ph.D., 13 March, 1989.

3. Arnold Abrams, "Faculty-Board Rift at Adelphi Widens: Trustees Refuse to Meet with Teachers," *Newsday,* 17 April, 1989.
4. Letter from Sheldon Weinig to Peter Diamandopoulos, (not dated).
5. Letter from M. Curt Meltzer to Peter Diamandopoulos, 27 September, 1991.
6. Max Savelle, "Democratic Government of the State University: A Proposal," *Bulletin of the American Association of University Professors,* Volume 43, Number 2, June 1957, p. 324.
7. Ibid., p. 325.
8. At its previous meeting on October 17, 1995, the Board of Trustees unanimously passed the following resolution:

> The Board of Trustees, after its careful review of the facts about Adelphi's conditions and practices, unequivocally reaffirms its confidence in the integrity and stewardship of Peter Diamandopoulos as President of Adelphi; and that

> The Board of Trustees reaffirms its policy actions over the last decade, directing the President's philosophical and practical turnaround of Adelphi; and that

> The Board directs the President to continue vigorously to take all steps necessary to advance the University towards the lofty and ambitious goals repeatedly articulated by the Board; and that

> The Board, in consequence of the foregoing, reaffirms the appropriateness of the compensation of the President for his achievements and record as the leader of the remarkable revival of Adelphi during his tenure, and for the purposes of securing his continuing commitment to the University.

> At the beginning of her report at a subsequent Board meeting on May 1, 1996, the chair of the Board stated: "I want to make mention of the fact that the University activities under the direction of our able President continue to operate at 'high-speed,' in spite of the deterrents which face us every day. He is to be commended for having the fortitude and vitality to endure the affronts by the many participants including the negative press. It is important that we continue to give the President our fullest support and cooperation."

9. Actually, a year later, on March 8, 1995, the Board decided that faculty were not making good use of sabbatical leaves, and with the recommendation of one of its committees "to postpone action on sabbatical requests by the faculty due to lack of standards," unanimously voted to withhold them:

> WHEREAS, the Board of Trustees, through its Academic Affairs Committee, considered the recommendation of the provost ad interim regarding the accomplishments of last year's sabbaticals, and the rationales for endorsing proposed new sabbaticals; and

> WHEREAS, the Board judged the documents presented unpersuasive and providing no grounds for endorsing the faculty's and the provost's recommendations,

NOW, THEREFORE, the Board of Trustees resolves to postpone action on sabbatical requests for 1995-96 until such time as sabbatical proposals have been strengthened to provide adequate detail regarding the academic merit of these proposals, including specific project objectives, careful and measurable plans of work, clear statements of the benefits of the project, and clear statements of expected outcomes.

Rightly or wrongly, faculty see sabbatical leaves as their due, and at least three Trustees who supported this resolution fully understood this. It is an object of wonderment why not a single Trustee could foresee that this unnecessary act of vindictiveness would only infuriate faculty and escalate the level of enmity on campus, nor attempt to head off more trouble, as many Trustees professed to be their wish.

10. Exhibit, P-274. According to these figures, the amounts varied from a high of $146,867 which was paid in 1989, to a low of $100,968, which was paid in 1987. A note at the bottom of this Exhibit suggests that these numbers may underestimate the amount of the commissions: "These figures are based on the attached summary of the insurance documents produced by respondents. The totals are approximate, as respondents did not provide complete commission information for all insurance policies issued to Adelphi University through E.G. Bowman."

11. Exhibit, R-12I.

12. *Vacco v. Diamandopoulos,* (and 17 other former Trustees), Sup Ct, New York County, 6 April, 1998, Ramos, J., Index No. 401253/97, paragraph 55, p. 15.

13. According to a survey of 475 private American colleges and universities, forty-six academic administrators earned more than $300,000 in the 1996-97 academic year. The ten institutions providing the highest compensations for their presidents were: Rockefeller University, $546,966; Vanderbilt University, $525,496; University of Pennsylvania, $514,878; Columbia University, $458,480; New York University, $451,643; Yale University, $447,265; Hofstra University, $438,554; Carnegie-Mellon University, $436,164; Johns Hopkins University, $435,592; and George Washington University, $425,041. In the 1995-96 academic year, thirty-eight academic administrators made more than $300,000. Academic administrators at large public universities make considerably less than their counterparts at private universities. For example, at the State University of New York, which has sixty-four campuses, the chancellor's salary was $250,000. Although salaries of presidents have been increasing faster than those of faculty, some of the latter—especially those with appointments in the professional schools: medicine, law, business, and engineering—earn more than $100,000 a year. (Karen W. Arenson, "In a 'Gilded Year' for University Presidents, Pay Moved Closer to the Board Room Level," *New York Times,* 18 October 1998, [New York Report], p. 30).

4

Lay Boards

The idea of lay trustees for institutions of higher learning can be traced back to the fourteenth century. In response to the excesses against faculty and townspeople by those enrolled in so-called student universities of the Bologna model, professors and city officials in Italy and Germany joined together to break the power of student guilds by appointing a board of curators to supervise teaching, administer grants for salaries, and control students.

Later, the doctrines of the Protestant Reformation gave both the church and state the responsibility to see that education was effective. Calvin believed that the greater the number of individuals involved in the governance of an institution, the more likely it would be self-corrective. He was convinced that the public interest would be best served through citizen involvement; the more participants, the more the benefits. More contemporary justifications of lay boards pretty much echo this view. James Conant contends that "the history of universities—in truth, of all human institutions, lay or clerical—proves by melancholy experience, that seminaries founded for the common weal, in the furtherance of sound knowledge, are, if left to themselves without an external and vigilant, and intelligent and disinterested supervision, regularly deflected from the great end for which they were created, and perverted to the private advantages of those through whom that end, it was confidently hoped, would be best accomplished."[1]

Calvin's Academy for higher studies which he founded in Geneva in 1559 was placed in the hands of representatives selected by the city government, and embodied his theory of lay control. This model was followed in other Reformation colleges—Leyden and Edinburgh—

established in the sixteenth century. Ownership and control were placed outside the institutions under civil and ecclesiastical supervision.

In 1650, the charter of Harvard College was changed to provide for two governing boards, one internal and the other external. By the eighteenth century, the latter of the two—the Board of Overseers— had effective authority over the College. The former—the President and Fellows of Harvard College—no longer even appointed those who were to serve as tutors.

Since the eighteenth century, virtually all institutions of higher learning in the United States have been governed by lay boards. The formal institutionalization of the practice reaches back to the New England and Mid-Atlantic colonies when laymen—most often clergy with some support from civic leaders—would create a college and turn its direction and supervision over to some of the organizers and others in the immediate community. The intention of the founders was to continue to have a hand in guiding the education of students by keeping the governing board, which they filled, separate from the instructional staff.

After the original trustees have been named to college boards in the act of incorporation, it has commonly been the practice for a board to become self-perpetuating.

Here is how Kirkpatrick describes the origins of what has become the American prototype of the lay board:

> We find the first example in Connecticut where the clergy were anxious to have a college more completely under their control than that of their neighbors next north of them.... The Yale charter provided for a permanent governing board which had no intention of acting, first or last, as a resident board of instruction. They proposed to employ the teachers and keep the direction of the school in their own hands. Similar conditions led to determining the form of Princeton's constitution and so also of King's, later to become Columbia.

> Another and perhaps more worthy consideration led to the confirmation of this precedent.... Teachers were scarce and had little or no professional standing or organization. Indeed, there were no such professional groups. Most of the teaching was done by young clergymen acting for a few years as tutors while they pursued their ministerial studies. Obviously, they were not in a position to organize and support, in its early days of struggle in pioneer communities, a college....[2]

As institutions of higher learning were founded in other colonies and across the country in the nineteenth and twentieth centuries, this model was copied and became nearly universally accepted. Faculty guilds that dominated Oxford and Cambridge Universities in England never took hold in America.

The methods for selecting members to the lay board are by charter, co-option, direct vote of a constituency, indirect election, appointment, *ex officio* designation, or inheritance. Given these various practices, it is generally a mistake to compare "a self-elected academic board responsible to itself with a board of bank directors elected by and responsible to the shareholders of the bank."[3] Yet, while the definition of the extent of the duties and the composition of the membership of lay boards slowly evolved over the last century as institutions of higher learning have become more complex, their function has come to be seen as resembling boards of directors of businesses or industries.

Lay boards have been established by statute, charter, legal decision, and practice. From almost the beginning and up to the present, the state has recognized the lay governing board as the college. This arrangement whereby they govern institutions of higher learning is thus supported by law and tradition.

Full control or ultimate and final authority over colleges and universities by a lay board is unusual in that it is virtually without parallel outside of the United States. In Europe, from which so many aspects of American higher education have been borrowed, faculty in part govern themselves. This is not to deny that in most countries there is sometimes official and unofficial involvement by the state. On the other hand, in the United States, members of the faculty of an institution are not only not a presence on boards, but often are prohibited by the charter or by-laws from membership. In 1810, a template was set at Columbia College:

> The said trustees, and their successors, shall forever hereafter have full power and authority to direct and prescribe the course of study and the discipline to be observed in the said college, and also to select and appoint by ballot or otherwise, a president of the said college, who shall hold his office during good behaviour; and such professor or professors, tutor or tutors, to assist the president in the government and education of the students belonging to the said college, and such other officer or officers, as to the said trustees shall seem meet, all of whom shall hold their offices during the pleasure of the trustees. *Provided always,* that no such professor, tutor, or other assistant officer shall be a trustee.[4]

Some institutions do permit faculty full board membership, and at times on some campuses faculty views may be sought, although this is often a mere courtesy or sop. Under the best of circumstances, faculty have a limited voice in many aspects of the decision-making process.

Since the early decades of the twentieth century, most members of governing boards are no longer drawn from the clergy; presently the majority have backgrounds in business, banking, politics, and the professions, particularly law. At a number of institutions of higher learning, one might find a few educators—generally a local college or university president, a distinguished alumnus or alumna, or renowned scholars or scientists—on a board. One purpose for these appointments is to provide some expertise on academic matters to the lay members.

Lay boards are often praised for the direct and indirect financial contributions many members make to a college or university. Moreover, they are said to give colleges and universities something less tangible: the collective wisdom of successful, socially and politically connected, and economically privileged men and women.

According to a 1989 report sponsored by the Association of Governing Boards of Universities & Colleges, lay trustees must "guard and care for the following":

- the overall and long-run welfare of the individual institution, including its specially chosen missions, and the best of its past and its brightest prospects for the future;

- the autonomy of the institution from outside bureaucratic, economic, and political domination;

- the academic freedom of the members of the community;

- the balance of the institution against single-minded demands of internal or external constituencies; and

- the public welfare in the general conduct of the institution, including the wise use of its resources and its adherence to high levels of academic behavior— assuring social responsibility and simultaneously protecting institutional autonomy.[5]

Under the law, the board defines institutional policies and procedures, oversees financial resources, and mediates between the institution and the community. Under the most ideal circumstances and at most, faculty primarily set the curriculum and the manner of teaching it, identify who will become permanent colleagues, and determine who will be granted degrees. Formally, the president's sphere is restricted to providing leadership in articulating an institution's ends and means and in publicly representing it. Here, much of the time, there is a huge gap between this conception and reality.

It is widely believed that the diversity, competition, growth, and robustness of American higher education is largely the result of the control of both private and public institutions of higher learning by lay boards. On occasion, boards have effectively acted as a buffer between, on the one hand, faculty and students and, on the other, those with power in society. They can and have served to reassure the public that despite faculty or student unrest or behavior deemed unacceptable in the wider community, the college or university is a safe place; it is in respectable and trustworthy hands.

Drawbacks

Notwithstanding the praise and benefits that the institution of lay boards may have brought to American higher education, there are also obvious problems that have been created by their unlimited power to make policy and see to its implementation. As Veblen saw it: "Governing boards of businessmen are quite useless.... The boards are of no material use in any connection; their sole effectual function being to interfere with the academic management of matters that are not of the nature of business, and lie outside their competence and outside of their habitual interest."[6] Abraham Flexner believed that lay boards "create an atmosphere of timidity which is not without effect in initial appointments and in promotions."[7]

At Adelphi, the by-laws state that "the Board of Trustees shall have control over the University and shall have and execute the corporate powers prescribed by said laws. Its primary function shall be policy making designed to insure the educational effectiveness and excellence of the University and [it should have] responsibilities for sound resource management of the corporation.... [It should also] determine the general educational, human resource and financial policies of the University..., [and within it resides] the power and function to carry them out." The considerable scope of this or any board's authority obviously limits that of the faculty's.

It is easy to see that giving power to lay boards, who might not have a full understanding of how to use it, in effect enhances the authority of a college or university president and his staff. This has important implications, as Stratton reminded us almost a century ago:

> The American university president holds a place unique in the history of higher education. He is a ruler responsible to no one whom he governs, and he holds

for an indefinite term the powers of academic life and death.... To the faculty, it is true, there seems to be left the important power to define the requirements for admission to the university and to its degrees, and yet these activities are in a fundamental way directed by the president, since by his word comes growth to this department and atrophy to that. And while his sway is subject to a constitution, and he cannot quite justly be called an autocrat, nevertheless the charter brings to him, perhaps, less serious restrictions than those which often in the larger world bind men who bear the name emperor.[8]

The situation is not that different on most campuses today than when this was written.

Having no special knowledge of the functioning of institutions of higher learning, a board must turn to and cede its power to academic administrators to oversee and operate the campus. The fact of lay boards creates the need for active, often strong, and involved college and university presidents with abundant staffs to whom administrative duties can be entrusted. It has long been known that this is pretty much inevitable:

Meetings of the board are infrequent, often but once a year and then perhaps in a city remote from the college they [sic] own and operate. They have little if any opportunity to inform themselves about conditions, even if they had, as very rarely they can have, the experience and knowledge which would enable them to decide wisely about difficult questions and to formulate effective policies. They must have an expert resident agent. That agent is the president.[9]

The campus president is put in the position to act for a board. To the majority of a governing board, he or she is the expert on academic matters. As a consequence, senior academic administrators do not simply carry out policy; they in large part set it. In overseeing and operating a campus, a president can bend board policy and actually establish a new or different agenda. Boards may control budgets, but academic administrators control the flow of information, and this can be decisive in how a budget is allocated. A campus president can fairly easily set or at least alter spending priorities. He or she can pretty much with impunity run roughshod over faculty wishes in fiscal matters.

As was noted in a 1920 report of the American Association of University Professors:

What happens in normal cases is as follows: Boards of trustees, being composed for the most part of busy men of affairs frequently possessing no special competence to pass judgment on matters of educational policy, rely chiefly upon the president for information and advice as to how things are going and what things should be done. Rarely does a board call in other members of the faculty for information and advice. *Thus the powers actually exercised by university presidents are, to a very great extent, not powers legally conferred upon the office by charters, but exercised by the incumbents of the office as surrogates for groups of busy men who are not educational experts, and, fortunately, in most cases know they are not.*[10]

If the president be a vigorous and dominating personality, he may thus become a force accelerating the dilution of educational ideals by gratifying the ambition to realize grandiose schemes.[11]

In brief, faculty are largely helpless in the face of administrative folly or capriciousness when it occurs, regardless of the latter's protestations to the contrary.

In the normal course of events, a board would be out of its element if it went much beyond considering the most general financial questions facing an institution. As the following exchange between the chair of the Board of Trustees and a member of the Regents' subcommittee makes clear, even "the simple principle that boards should legislate and presidents should execute"[12] did not hold at Adelphi.

Ernesta Procope:

Q[from Regent]: Did the Board of Trustees establish annual goals for the University?

A: For the University as a whole?

Q: Yes.

A: We had financial goals.

Q: The University as a whole in different categories?

A: The President may have had that himself.

Q: Did the Board of Trustees establish annual goals for the University?

A: Only financial goals, as I recall.

Q: It did not establish goals as far as student recruitment is concerned?

A: No, it did not.

Q: Recruitment of faculty?

A: No, but we have reports from various chairmen of committees.

Q: That's not what I'm asking you. Program enhancement?

A: Yes.

Q: You established goals?

A: The Board did not establish those goals.

Q: I'm asking if the Board established them.

A: They were established by administration and shared with us for our approval.

Q: Did the Board approve the budget for Adelphi University?

A: Yes.

Q: Was the budget related to the goals of the University?

A: To the financial goals, yes.

Q: Is that all the Board of Trustees looked at, the financial goals, it did not look at any of the other goals?

A: It looks at the goals that the President has set forth for the various departments of the University, without a doubt. (Testimony, pp. 1329-31)

The less familiar governing boards are with academic matters, the greater the necessity of having to follow the lead of academic administrators.

One dimension of a common classification of social power is expert power, controlling essential knowledge or information.[13] With the single exception of the investment of endowment, very few members of a board could possibly know as much about academic life as a campus president and other senior administrators. They would not be expected to know more. This fact alone would give academic administrators a certain authority vis-à-vis a governing board. Moreover, it is generally the campus president and his staff that keep the institution moving, not members of the governing board. And since power can also be defined as the ability to get things done, it is something given to academic administrators which they are expected to use.

Insufficient Knowledge

The institution of lay boards creates a number of other problems for higher education. Most central is that many of their members are almost completely uninformed about the basic facts of academic life, and it is difficult to see, as Veblen suggests, what they could contribute to governing institutions of higher learning. The following example from an influential board member of Adelphi University demonstrates how little some know. In this exchange, it would appear that the chair of the Board knows less than any parent of a college-age student about the range of educational options open to undergraduates.

Ernesta Procope:

Q: Do you know whether or not there are rating services that rate, from a student's perspective, the value of an education at different institutions?

A: I don't know....

Q: Do you know whether or not there are publishing companies that publish books that would describe, from a student's perspective, the value of an education at different institutions of higher learning?

A: I would think so.

Q: Do you know of any particular books that are published?

A: No, I don't....

Q: Do you know how Adelphi has been rated by the books that are published concerning the value of an education from a student's perspective?

A: I would think rather high.

Q: Excuse me?

A: I would think rather high.

Q: Well, I'm—

A: I've never seen anything in writing.

Q: I don't want to ask you your speculation. I'm asking you what you have read or know about. Do you know how Adelphi is rated by any magazine that rates on an annual basis?...

A: No. (Testimony, pp. 742-45)

The apparent incomprehension here may sound extreme, but it is not that unusual or necessarily unexpected. A lay governing board "belongs neither to those who study nor to those who teach, and is in consequence disjoined from the real life of the institution. Often their high character, their training, their devotion to the work, greatly reduces the disjunction, yet is the separation real."[14]

Other Expertise

To offset their less than full understanding of so many particulars of institutions of higher learning, lay board members may rely on colleagues with academic backgrounds for direction. This may not always work to their advantage. The Adelphi Board of Trustees often turned to the controversial president of Boston University, John Silber, for advice. However, his suggestions were so consistently idiosyncratic, the Board appears to have made decisions that were as likely to exacerbate problems as to lead to solutions. In reviewing the following comments by Silber, it should be recalled that at the center of the Committee to Save Adelphi's charges against the Board of Trustees was that President Diamandopoulos's salary and benefits package was excessive and that his management style was dictatorial. The latter was most evident in the administration's unilateral decisions to cut programs that resulted in decreasing enrollments and revenues.

Silber sees himself as someone especially qualified in matters of higher education. To the question: "Do you consider yourself an expert in education and in educational administration, Dr. Silber?," he responded: "Yes" (Testimony, pp. 1722-23). In rejecting a suggestion by a Regent that speedy resolutions of administrative-faculty conflict is usually a wise course of action, Silber responded: "And to exhort me to be aware of the problem, I find somewhat strange. Because I think I'm about as acutely and articulately aware of the problem as anyone alive" (Testimony, p. 2018).

Silber was able to convince others that this self-characterization was accurate. He had had some success in fundraising as an academic administrator, which impressed many of his colleagues on the Adelphi Board. With his forceful personality, he was not reluctant to express a wide range of opinions on academic matters which he represented as fact. His actual knowledge falls well short of his self-assessment and self-assurance. Here he explains his views on presidential compensation and on academic governance to the subcommittee of Regents.

John Silber(on presidential compensation):

Q: Do you believe that compensation should be related in any way to the endowment of the institution?

A: Yes. The lower the endowment, the harder it is to do the job, and, therefore, the higher the salary should be. (Testimony, p. 1591)

A: We need him. We definitely need him. It's because of his academic talent that you want to lock him in. And if you want to know why you have to raise his pay, it is because of the abuse he's taken.... And I'm trying to understand why you suppose that you know better than the Trustees of Adelphi University who use a businessman's judgment on this matter, that you know better than they that he shouldn't be paid that much. (Testimony, p. 2005-6)

Although it would appear that Adelphi's Board was guided by these principles, at least one Regent found Silber's comments on presidential compensation perplexing:

When I went to college [Yale University] we had a new president, Kingman Brewster, who came in when I was in law school, and I remember his opening statement to the students was he had a plan for dealing with the three essential components of university life, as he viewed it, and he identified those three components as the alumni, the students, and the faculty. Your theory of compensation for a university president appears to be that if that president not only does not get along well with one of the major segments of the team of the university, namely, the faculty, but indeed is defamed and pilloried, your words, that the president ought to be more compensated rather than less compensated, should be more locked in for lifetime security rather than less locked in, and that theory of compensation I find fascinating because it runs up against everything that I have been taught. (Testimony, pp. 1987-88)

The Regent later asked: "Why do we need to continue this? What is the Board doing by giving additional incentives to him to continue a situation that is hurting that fine institution?" (Testimony, p.2007).

John Silber (on academic governance):

A: I think that one of the things that we have done there that made the decision not to accept the usurpation of administrative authority ... [is] we have moved ahead to the development of the Honors College over their [the faculty's] objection. We are moving ahead with regard to the revisions in the School of Business over the objections of some of the faculty, not necessarily the Dean of the School of Business, but of the Faculty Senate again. We are in the process of making clear to them that the administration of the University is the respon-

sibility of the administration, that while the faculty share and share very substantially in the administration, they do share management. They share management in the selection of students, they select management, they share management in the consideration of courses and in the offering of courses, in the
evaluation of students, in the evaluation of faculty members, and their recommendations of which faculty members should be considered for sabbaticals and
so forth, and for promotion. All of those are managerial functions that are
shared by the faculty with the administration. But there are other objectives
that are the primary prerogatives of the administration. And at that point, we
expect the faculty to be cooperative in the realization of those goals.

Q[from Regent]: Is my understanding of the faculty to be cooperative, is that
the faculty do it the president's way and the administration's way?

A: On certain issues and certain objectives—

Q: The ones that you have identified?

A: I think that is their responsibility. If they don't want to work in a university
that has this honors program, if they do not wish to work for a university that
has a core curriculum, if they find this in some way objectionable to their own
principles, then there is a wide road out there that they can take to go some-
place else or do something else. But they don't have the right to subvert the
institution on which their livelihood depends....

A: And it was only after [President Diamandopoulos] has extended his hand in
friendship to the faculty, time and time again, and [was] hit, slapped, and bitten
and chopped at, that he finally reached the point of accepting the position that
the Board of Trustees hold, that it is time to exercise the administrative and
managerial responsibility of the Trustees and insist that there be a responsible
performance, a professional performance, by the faculty of this University, one
supportive of its mission and one consistent with its flourishing. (Testimony,
pp. 1954-61)

A: You can't always appease people and succeed. I think you can learn that
from the 1930s. You don't appease certain power mad individuals simply by
acceding to them. There is some point at which the authority, the proper
authority that has been entrusted to the Board of Trustees of Adelphi, has to be
recognized and has to be exercised. (Testimony, pp.2018-19)

It is difficult to believe that Silber did not regularly share these
beliefs with other Trustees. It is not difficult to understand why the
New York State Board of Regents concluded that at Adelphi "there has
been a complete breakdown of the principles of governance, which the
Board of Trustees seems to countenance." The Trustees could hardly be
expected to ignore or transcend the expert advice they were offered.
Surely, other lay boards, past and present, would have done the same.

There are many compelling arguments against faculty running institutions of higher learning. One is that those most committed to academic work would have little interest in the tedium of day-to-day management and leave it in the hands of the less able; mediocre academics with a need to succeed at something would drift towards administration.

Flexner believed that without instituting democracy on campus, faculty should be represented in academic governance, but "should not be overburdened." He suggested that a campus "president is a good device," but added the warning that "he should not alone come between the faculty and the trustees."[15] Unfortunately, by design, this is precisely what happened at Adelphi, preventing the Board from attending to its obligations as set forth by the Association of Governing Boards of Universities & Colleges. It resulted in the New York State Board of Regents concluding that the Adelphi Board of Trustees had granted President Diamandopoulos pay and benefits far in excess of what other college and university presidents receive, that it did so without properly evaluating his job performance (that it had acted "blindly, recklessly, and heedlessly" in setting his remuneration), that two Trustees improperly profited by doing business with the University, and that it fostered a breakdown of collegial governance.

Shared Governance

The ambiguity inherent in boards, administration, and faculty sharing some of the same responsibilities of institutions of higher learning can often lead to conflict over large and small issues.

The principles of governance that guide almost all colleges and universities call for discrete yet interlocking functions for governing boards, the administration, and faculty. In effect, this attempt to promote shared governance creates both overlapping and fuzzy boundaries. In addition, the three bodies commonly have different interests. A further stumbling block is that it is sometimes unclear in exactly whose sphere some matters properly belong. By itself, any one of these factors can lead to tension or even friction; a combination inevitably will, as was the case at Adelphi.

The most widely recognized and central faculty rights revolve around academic concerns, anything related to educational policies and procedures. It is generally acknowledged that here faculty are particularly qualified to contribute to institutional governance. Indeed, much of the time, the faculty is involved in evaluating the qualifications of its members in decisions on appointments, promotions, and the granting of tenure; in participating in the selection of some academic administrators; in meeting with the administration on academic matters; in setting the curriculum; and in recommending academic standards for students.

In the end, however, the actions of governing boards are most critical. Their fiscal priorities largely circumscribe what else happens on a college or university campus. The desires of those with control over the expenditure of money have consequences for those with responsibilities over other functions; the reverse is very seldom true. If there are no funds available to expand some aspect of the curriculum no matter how much the faculty believe it is justified or necessary, it will not become part of the academic program. It could not possibly be otherwise. As Creighton cautioned, "it is clear that this [faculty] power can only extend a little way, unless it includes a voice in determining how the funds of the university are to be applied. Educational questions, and questions regarding the proper expenditure of money, can not be dissociated."[16] Faculty do not control budgets. For this reason they have a great deal less power than most are willing to concede.

The Faculty's Contribution to the Chaos

The realization that faculty are excluded from full participation in the most important matters or that their recommendations may be casually disregarded can be a source of considerable unhappiness, at least on the part of some. It does not take much goading to make faculty feel deprived of their rights. A dissatisfied faculty—even if only a minority—can torment administrators and those colleagues who do not share their penchant for activism. They can spread gossip, they can contact those in the media who delight in reporting whispers. They can go well beyond these more moderate steps. They can, as they did at Adelphi, hire private investigators to go through the trash of the president.[17] In short, they can cause a great deal of mischief and pain—and waste a good deal of time and energy, theirs and others.

Here are two example, from the same academic year, of the faculty leadership on Adelphi's troubled campus taking actions that were hardly sober, and which made no positive contribution to the University.

In early October 1995, the Faculty Senate passed a resolution designed to reverse changes being made to the curriculum of the School of Business and Management. In the view of the faculty, no course of study could in any way be altered without their consent, which they had never been asked to give. The faculty believed it was incumbent upon them to advise students that classes not approved by departmental or other faculty bodies "shall not be counted as part of the students' overall degree requirements."

In response, President Diamandopoulos characterized "this resolution [as part of an] irresponsible campaign." Concerned that what they had done would unnecessarily penalize students, the faculty proposed a substitute motion requesting that the union file a grievance, and urging "all faculty to advise their students to avoid registering for these courses based on a list generated by the Faculty Senate listing all courses not approved by the faculty." The senior vice president's reaction was less measured than the President's:

> It must be obvious that to sow doubt among students about the integrity of their classes is irresponsible, harmful to our students, and damaging to the University. Consequently, I want there to be no mistake in this serious matter: any member of the faculty who, in advising students about their courses or in teaching assigned classes, conveys the idea that a course appearing in the official class schedule and being offered by any unit of the University as authorized by the Board of Trustees will not count as part of the students' degree requirements, will be subject to the full range of appropriate sanction for irresponsible faculty behavior.

The unpleasantness surrounding the School of Business and Management's curriculum resurfaced the following semester. At the close of the January 29, 1996 Faculty Senate meeting, the following motion was proposed:

> Whereas the faculty of the School of Management and Business voted in May 1995 to halt implementation of the [new undergraduate management] program, and not to offer courses that had not been approved; and
>
> Whereas the Faculty Senate academic affairs committee has not approved the proposed new undergraduate management program in the School of Management and Business; and
>
> Whereas the Faculty Senate has not approved that proposed program;
>
> The Senate hereby disapproves the proposed new undergraduate program in management, and urges, in the strongest terms, that the President immediately

reinstate the...[previous] programs...until such time as a new undergraduate curriculum receives approval by the Faculty Senate, as required by the governance documents.

On February 12, the departing dean of the School of Business, speaking against the motion, appealed to the Faculty Senate to support what everyone agreed were necessary and overdue changes in the curriculum:

> Speeches are seen as self-serving, and I have 15 days remaining here, so I have no self-serving interest in your debate. I ask you not to hurt the students, the only ones who will be hurt and shouldn't be.

> My chronology of events: Two years before I arrived, in 1991-92, there was a committee in the School of Business, which was working on a new curriculum for the undergraduate program at the request of the provost. Enrollment had declined, and the curriculum wasn't responsive to the needs of a changing business world.... The committee met regularly (weekly) to produce philosophy and curriculum. We presented developments to open meetings of faculty...throughout 1992-93. In 1993, the Board requested external evaluators, and appointed them, [and they] recommended severe revisions of the undergraduate curriculum.... By April 1994, the faculty brought in the structure of the new BBA and two new courses, which was voted in 17 to 12, and the courses 21 to 7....

> Faculty approved the structure and course disciplines on June 6, 1994. Shortly thereafter the packet was forwarded to the FSCAA [Faculty Senate Committee on Academic Affairs] for review, and to the New York State Department of Education for their information. We were not putting in a new program, but were revising/changing an approved curriculum, so we needed no approval.... We were simply notifying them.

> We were given approval to go ahead with the two new courses. Eidson was the new chair of FSCAA, and FSCAA didn't meet. Nothing happened. FSCAA wanted only program changes, but we went to them as a courtesy. Over the summer, faculty worked on new courses, which were offered in fall 1994 by Geiss and Gupta. In spring 1995, things began to fall apart. I decided to change the structure of the school, which I should have done soon after I came. After two and a half years, it was perceived as a power play rather than revitalization.

> The Faculty Senate made a motion to disapprove. I, as dean, informed the faculty that we would go ahead with the new curriculum despite no faculty approval. In 1995-96, faculty were assigned to teach new courses. Faculty were directed to teach, or disciplinary action would follow. A grievance is proceeding. I assigned faculty again in 1996, with no new grievance.

> Ask business faculty why this motion [expressing disapproval of the proposed new undergraduate program, and urging reinstatement of the outdated one] was

put forward. Students are enrolled, with about 100 students in their second year of evolution. The old curriculum is, very bluntly, not responsive to the needs of the community. This group [the Senate] should direct the faculty...to get busy and develop the program which they already approved 21 to 7. We got into a process debate which makes us look like asses while the students are ignored.

No matter what you do, it will have no impact—except to hurt and confuse our students and hurt Adelphi. The only harm is to our students, who are paying for a modern education. We aren't fighting over good or bad curriculum, but an interpretation of process! Some courses are being taught without sufficient development, while the faculty is instead engaging in a process fight. This is insane. The old program ain't good, we can't go back, it won't work. We'll only confuse students. Courses taken *will* count toward graduation. The Board *will* approve, and grant degrees. The Board hires faculty and certifies courses; the faculty doesn't. You are just hurting students. Think about our 300+ students..., and do what is right for them. Direct the business faculty to get back to work.

The discussion after the dean's mostly evenhanded and earnest appeal was superficial. Many comments were not even responsive to the issues he had raised. Rather than exchange ideas and engage in serious debate, most Senate members chose to vent their anger and suspicions. Unfounded assertions ("I realized the administration wasn't serious.... Administration doesn't support the commitment of quality programs, and they want appearance only.") were not called into question. When there were relevant criticisms, the dean's attempt to address them fell on deaf ears.

There was an evident absence of concentrated intelligence. The faculty did not seem to be listening, and remained unyielding. As the charade continued, the discourse became more surreal: "[The dean] has been efficient in painting those faculty involved as having an agenda to hurt students. I can't believe my peers would do so." The motion passed with no dissent. The faculty had again shown the Adelphi administration that it could vote to resist it.

In the second instance, the executive committee of the Faculty Senate was invited to meet with three senior administrators in the last week of February 1996 to discuss the "potential implications" of unfavorable enrollment projections; the administration was concerned about the "structure of the institution and the fiscal-academic issues confronting Adelphi." Faculty, who had already been apprised of the problem, were asked for "suggestions as to how the University could deal with a substantial projected revenue shortfall." Members of the Faculty Senate offered little in the way of suggestions.

Within a week, however, the president of the faculty union wrote the administration stating that "this meeting qualifies as an initial consultation with the Faculty Senate to determine 'whether a financial exigency exists' under Article XV of the *Collective Bargaining Agreement*. As such, we would like to begin the independent financial audit guaranteed us under the language of the contract in Article XV. With time being a crucial variable in these deliberations, we will contact you within 10 days with the name of the independent auditor we will use, and a list of the financial, enrollment, admissions, and planning documents we will require."

In response, the senior vice president assured the chair of the Faculty Senate that "I specifically indicated to you that this [financial exigency] was a situation that, as a 'worst case scenario,' the University was seeking all means to avoid. We are, clearly, not in a situation of financial exigency. Rather, we face serious potential enrollment declines." He repeated this in a memorandum to the faculty union president. Instead of acknowledging a misunderstanding and extending a hand to work with the administration on the problem, she brusquely reminded the vice president:

> Even absent a financial exigency, the faculty through the Senate has primary responsibility for matters pertaining to the academic policies of the University and is entitled to advise University with respect to major budgetary issues. Accordingly, I trust that you will abide by the terms of the Articles of Governance and fully include the faculty, through the Senate, in decisions bearing on those issues.

The following day, the vice president wrote once more explaining that it was precisely faculty consultation that led him to call the meeting in the first place.

Again, the Adelphi faculty and administration failed to work together on an issue of concern to both, and to students. Academic life at Adelphi was not enhanced, nor was the principle of shared governance.

There were numerous documented reasons why faculty at Adelphi might be skittish of the administration. Nonetheless, their inflexibility and insistence on the administration's pliancy surely prodded Diamandopoulos to greater acts of imperiousness.

In the last analysis, the academic system is hierarchical. Boards have ultimate authority; legally, in any disagreement, their word is conclusive. What faculty say or want is never more than a recommendation. When faculty, after repeatedly being ignored or rebuffed, can no longer deny this, a breakdown in the pretense of shared power and in a modicum of mutual trust and collegiality is not uncommon. The results are a constant sense of grievance and perpetual strife, as the above two examples clearly illustrate. Creighton was aware that this eventuality could infect academic life:

> In universities, as in all social organizations, absolute power is the weakest form of authority, because it is exclusive and disintegrating. In denying the rights of others, it establishes a system of potential war, where there is no law but the will of the strongest.[18]

Attempts to resolve a governance dispute in academia by determining who has moral authority or tradition on his side introduces other considerations, some spurious and some legitimate, and all peripheral. Most importantly, who may have appeared to have gained the high ground will have little impact on what ultimately is done.

It is a faculty conceit to view themselves as being more central and influential in decision making than what reality would suggest. These unrealistic expectations often end in chronic bruised feelings, and, of course, discord.

Many who have served on governing boards have recognized this truth and have advised colleagues to take steps to avoid potential friction. Board members have been cautioned not to get too involved in campus affairs by second-guessing administration or faculty. A member of the Harvard governing board counseled new colleagues "I can sum up the [rules of conduct that must be followed] by a big 'don't'—DON'T MEDDLE.... As I see it, the job of a lay member of a governing board...boils down to this: Do your best to see that the organization is good, that it is well manned, and that it runs smoothly —but don't try to run it."[19] A committee of the board of Columbia University also recommended restraint: "The most experienced trustees are themselves constantly warning their newer colleagues that overactivity in certain areas—particularly in the area of education itself—is as great a sin against the modern spirit of trusteeship as neglect."[20] Heeding such warnings can keep resentment from boiling to the surface. The Board at Adelphi, unduly impressed by the President and persuaded by those colleagues who insisted that he was always right and that the faculty were always wrong and that his hopes could easily become reality, failed to do this. The consequence was an odd combination sometimes of personal pathology and public dramatics and sometimes of personal dramatics and public pathology.

One last conclusion here seems fairly obvious: if one accepts the precept that some degree of consensus is necessary to avoid continuous conflict, then the combination of lay boards and the appearance of shared governance seems to be a recipe that would preclude this. Moreover, as it has been pointed out, final authority rests with the trustees: "they may abdicate from their position of authority, but they cannot annul it; they may vacate their posts, but they cannot destroy them; they may delegate activities and decisions, but they cannot thereby avoid their own responsibilities."[21] These facts make the idea of shared governance inherently unstable. At the minimum, events at Adelphi University might lead one to examine this question.

Notes

1. James B. Conant, *Academic Patronage and Superintendence,* Cambridge, MA: Harvard University Press, 1953, p. 37.
2. John E. Kirkpatrick, *Force and Freedom in Education,* Yellow Springs, OH: The Antioch Press, 1929, pp. 65-66.
3. John E. Kirkpatrick, *The American College and Its Rulers,* New York: New Republic, Inc., 1927, p. 91.
4. As quoted in J. McKeen Cattell, *University Control,* New York and Garrison, NY: The Science Press, 1913, p. 11.
5. Clark Kerr and Marian L. Gade, *The Guardians: Boards of Trustees of American Colleges and Universities, What They Do and How Well They Do It,* Washington, DC: Association of Governing Boards of Universities & Colleges, 1989, p. 12. To emphasize the seriousness of the matter, the study goes on to outline seven specific tasks:

    - selecting, advising, supporting, and evaluating the president;
    - establishing major policies, including approval of the budget and important new programs, and reviewing and evaluating the performance of the institution in all its major aspects — including academic areas;
    - participating in representing the institution to the surrounding society and in obtaining resources;
    - supervising investment, legal affairs, and buildings and grounds;
    - acting as a "court of last resort" to internal conflicts;
    - being willing and able to fill gaps in performance by other elements of the institution in emergency situations and then to withdraw when the special circumstance no longer exists — the "in reserve" function; and
    - encouraging adaptation and renewal of the institution to make it more useful and to avoid stagnation and retrogression (pp. 12-13).

6. Thorstein Veblen, *The Higher Learning in America: A Memorandum on the Conduct of Universities by Business Men,* New York: B.W. Huebsch, 1918, p. 66.
7. Abraham Flexner, *Universities: American, English, German,* New York: Oxford University Press, 1930, p. 180.

8. George M. Stratton, "Externalism in American Universities," *Atlantic Monthly,* Volume 100, Number 4, October 1907, pp. 513-14.
9. John E. Kirkpatrick, *The American College and Its Rulers,* p. 114.
10. J. A. Leighton (Chairman), "Report of Committee T on Place and Function of Faculties in University Government and Administration," *Bulletin of the American Association of University Professors,* Volume 6, Number 1, January 1920, p. 19.
11. Ibid., p. 20.
12. Edward C. Elliott, M. M. Chambers, and William A. Ashbrook, *The Government of Higher Education: Designed for the Use of University and College Trustees,* New York: American Book Company, 1935, p. 187.
13. John R. P. French, Jr., and Bertram Raven, "The Bases of Social Power," in Dorwin Cartwright, Editors, *Studies in Social Power,* Ann Arbor, Michigan: The University of Michigan, Research Center for Group Dynamics, Institute for Social Research, 1959.
14. Stratton, "Externalism in American Universities," p. 513.
15. Flexner, *Universities,* pp. 184-85.
16. J. E. Creighton, "The Government of American Universities," *Science,* August 12, 1910.
17. Academic administrators—not only public officials, those engaged in criminal activities, and celebrities—can leave incriminating or embarrassing paper trails, and these can lead to explosive revelations. Among other things found in President Diamandopoulos's refuse was a copy of a fax that he and his wife sent to Trustee John Silber at a Hong Kong hotel referring to a number of crank, obscene telephone calls they had made to a faculty union leader that were recorded on the voice-mail system. In the first, the shortest, a male was heard: "Fuck you" was his simple message. The woman was more expansive in six other: Number three commanded: "Shove your Save Your Adelphi Committee up your ass." Number four had a political theme: "I thought that I was calling the Committee to Save Adelphi. What is the AAUP [American Association of University Professors]? I thought you were some liberal ass-wiping, you know radical, Nazi, sort of you know, Karl Marx crap organization, that's, you know, hanging around and destroying our universities. I want you out of there, not President Diamandopoulos." In one, no one spoke. In another there was simply the unmistakable sound of a toilet flushing.
   The note to Silber boasted: "Petros thought you would find some prurient interest in the forthcoming documents. We both left a few choice, but well-beneath-our-dignity, messages on their voice mail this evening. Petros said the war was on. However, I believe not enough blood has been shed to commence a proper battle...."
   When asked about the matter, Silber acknowledged that he was registered at the hotel on the date the fax was sent, but that he had never received it. "In my opinion it is a forgery," he responded. "I don't believe the fax was ever sent." The records of the hotel's night manager indicated that it had been delivered to Silber's room. To this, Silber suggested "it's possible the maid picked it up and threw it away." Diamandopoulos said that he was "mystified and perplexed" by the entire business, and that it was "inconceivable" that his wife was in some way involved. A month later, the AAUP employee to whom the calls were directed sent a transcript of the messages and wrote to Trustee Silber asking him to look into the incident:

> I have reason to believe that the calls were placed by individuals in or con-
> nected with the University administration. I am sure that you will agree with
> me that this type of discourse is highly inappropriate in a university commu-
> nity.

> I am writing to you [the Board] in your capacity as fiduciaries of the University
> to urge you to conduct an immediate investigation... .

The letter was ignored. (Also ignored was a most important ethical question of
what the faculty or those whom they had hired were doing in the President's
trash.) Actually, a month later Silber made reference to the letter to two journal-
ists for a newsmagazine preparing an article on the incident.

> I am in receipt of a faxed transmission apparently addressed to me in Hag
> Kong (note: it is not addressed to Hong Kong, but to Hag Kong). It purports to
> be from Petros and Maria Diamandopoulos....

> I never received a fax of this nature from anyone and certainly not from Mr.
> and Mrs. Diamandopoulos.

> The very first sentence in this message is so deeply insulting that I would have
> been outraged to have received it. Consider, "Petros thought you would find
> some prurient interest in the forthcoming documents." I don't take a prurient
> interest in anything and would be deeply offended by the suggestion.

> I enclose a letter from a faculty member at Adelphi alleging the existence of
> anonymous telephone calls of an abusive and occasionally obscene nature. It
> was addressed to me as a member of the Board of Trustees, and the writer
> made what I consider to be the libelous suggestion that the telephone calls were
> from the administration and that, as a Trustee, I should make an investigation
> of them.

> I find troubling coincidence in this letter from one of the protesting faculty of
> Adelphi and the obviously bogus fax transmission you sent me. This appears to
> be part and parcel of an attempt by someone to falsify the record in order to
> damage Peter Diamandopoulos....

The evidence was then turned over to the Nassau County district attorney's office
to investigate aggravated-harassment charges. There was no indictment, and the
matter was eventually dropped.

18. Creighton, "The Government of American Universities," p. 400.
19. Special Trustee Committee, *The Role of the Trustees of Columbia University,*
    New York: New York Times, 1957, pp. 23-24.
20. Ibid., p. 9.
21. Beardsley Ruml, *Memo to a College Trustee,* New York: McGraw-Hill, 1959, pp.
    3-4.

5

The Work of the Academic Governing Board

There is considerably more praise than criticism of academic governing boards. From time to time, public board members are faulted for not being independent enough of the political leaders who appointed them. From the faculty's perspective, governing boards have a far from perfect record of defending the autonomy and academic freedom of individuals during times of political turmoil. Mostly, however, governing boards are held in high regard primarily for the altruism of their members.

Looking beyond the intentions of individual Trustees, this chapter considers how the Adelphi Board handled its responsibilities; how the Board did what governing boards are supposed to do is examined in some detail. Obviously, what is found cannot be applied to all lay governing boards, but surely some of it goes beyond the single case of Adelphi.

As we saw in chapter 4, the specific, fundamental tasks of academic governing boards are: (1) selecting campus presidents; (2) evaluating how well they and their administrations are performing; and (3) overseeing institutions' finances and resources—passing on budgets, helping them to remain solvent, and supervising investments.[1] This would appear to be straightforward enough, and, given the background of many governing board members, not unfamiliar or especially challenging. Most have had some experience assessing the work of others and in money matters—in commerce, in the public sector, or as professionals.

President Diamandopoulos believed that this third task was of uppermost importance. A few weeks after a retreat of the Adelphi Trustees held on March 1, 1986, he advised the entire Board that "the responsibilities of the Trustees...are to provide money and energy, and the commitment to engage in matters of the Board." In case anyone missed it, the point was reiterated later in the meeting: "In order for...the University to move ahead, Dr. Diamandopoulos outlined the following requisites: ...insuring the responsibility of the Board and the President to raise funds...."

Generally, academic governing boards spend a considerable amount of time discussing budgets and buildings. In light of the limited knowledge of most members about academic culture and institutions of higher learning, it would be expected that boards would focus on that about which the majority know most—issues related to finances.

Although members of the Adelphi Board were generally aware of their fiduciary and oversight duties, their actions were sometimes counterproductive to their effectively serving the University. This began when the Board decided to hire Diamandopoulos who had not done well in a previous appointment as a university president. Since it is relevant to any assessment of the Board's performance, the matter must be looked at carefully.

Selecting a President

If a governing board takes the shadow for the substance when choosing a president, it greatly increases the probability that it and the institution in its charge will soon face unnecessary and unexpected problems. This is what happened at Adelphi.

A committee for the 1984-85 Adelphi Board of Trustees spent months searching for a President for the University. After considerable time and money, it identified and recommended Peter Diamandopoulos; the entire Board agreed that he was the best of several candidates, and it voted to offer him the position.

Diamandopoulos's record as an academic administrator was readily available, and in light of this, the decision of the Board is perplexing.[2] If nothing else, it strongly suggests there must be other lay boards that also make grievous mistakes in selecting academic administrators. Surely, the Adelphi Board cannot be the only academic governing board, past or present, with little understanding of what it takes to run an institution of higher learning. (There is only limited, anecdotal evidence which would support the contention that some governing board members seem to have very little idea of what they are doing when assessing candidates for a college or university presidency.[3] The best evidence would be how well those whom they select perform.)

When Diamandopoulos was hired as the President of Adelphi, it would be difficult to conclude that the Board of Trustees closely examined or reflected on the very public record of his turbulent six-year presidency at Sonoma State University in California between 1977 and 1983. Here is the Adelphi Board chair's recollection of part of a conversation during negotiations prior to Diamandopoulos's appointment:

James T. Byrne, Jr.:

> Look, you know, we know what your credentials say; we know what your experience has been at your other institutions, but, you know, you're an unproven product and we're an unproven product. (Testimony, p. 5135)

This is untrue. Diamandopoulos was not an unproven product, an unknown quantity. He had been tested. He had shown himself to be anything but a successful academic administrator; given his erratic and confrontational management style, there was a high probability that his performance at Adelphi would be much like his performance at Sonoma State University.

Even if some Adelphi Trustees were looking for someone reputed to be a hard-nosed manager to rein in unrestrained spending or an unruly faculty, as some faculty contend, it is truly a mystery why the Board would settle on an individual whose poor judgment and recalcitrance as an academic administrator had so recently created so much chaos, and who had accomplished so little.[4]

It is not likely that it was simply Diamandopoulos's reputation of forcefulness that made him attractive to the Adelphi Board. Indeed, if it was convinced that belligerence or pugnacity, without accomplishment, was a positive quality that would serve Adelphi, this in itself would be grounds to conclude that some lay boards have no business governing institutions of higher learning. A brief review of Diamandopoulos's record at Sonoma State should have convinced any board, knowing what it was doing—whatever changes it would hope or expect to be implemented—that the chances were quite high that he would soon be at loggerheads with the faculty—and that there would be more bickering than governance at Adelphi, that he would push Adelphi to the brink as he did Sonoma State.

Diamandopoulos's Years at Sonoma State

With considerable fanfare, in the summer of 1977, Diamandopoulos became President at Sonoma State College, which is located about forty miles north of San Francisco and close to the city of Santa Rosa. Sonoma State was established in 1960 and began operating the following year with fewer than 300 students. It was one of the growing number of campuses of the California State College System, all of which were designated universities in 1978, the year after Diamandopoulos's arrival.

Sonoma's undergraduate program, which emphasized the liberal arts, attracted students from all parts of California. During the 1960s, the school grew steadily, reaching a peak of over 5,000 full-time students in 1974. By the time Diamandopoulos assumed office, it was facing declining enrollments and attendant cuts in budget and personnel.

Diamandopoulos's immoderate inauguration in September — he believed it important that the occasion be marked with "appropriate pomp and ceremony"—drew criticism from a vocal minority of Sonoma's undergraduates and faculty. These detractors questioned whether California taxpayers should bear the costs for what they saw as unnecessary and frivolous self-promotion. They pointed to the precarious financial state of the College which was facing staff cutbacks and possible layoffs of tenured faculty. Among other things, they noted that funding for the library had been reduced, and that a growing number of students and faculty were becoming frustrated and demoralized.

A flier was circulated on campus which stated that the event was "out of keeping with Sonoma State College which scorns exhibitions of elitism." It concluded that the ceremony was "distasteful, unethical, and very simply, unjustifiable." Diamandopoulos ignored the flap.

From the outset, Diamandopoulos's affectations had estranged a small nucleus of colleagues; they saw him as superficial and pretentious—"slow in realizing...[that] the divine right of kings died last century."

Diamandopoulos was not the first or the last academic or academic administrator to confuse pomposity and erudition. Yet, until 1980, his braggadocio engendered as much wonder as anger at Sonoma State. Those not captivated by his curious style were baffled by it. He was caricatured as often as he was attacked. He was celebrated, after a fashion, in a roundelay:

> and on this farm grew flowery prose
> ee i ee i o
> with philosophy here
> and priorities there
> here a plan
> there a goal
> all to save our tenured folk
> Diamandopoulos had a farm
> ee i ee i o
>
> and on this farm was a Greek mystique
> ee i ee i o
> with a Greek freak here....

In a short time, this gentle mocking evolved into unceasing conflict between Diamandopoulos and Sonoma State's faculty.

Diamandopoulos spent a good deal of time during his first few years at Sonoma State writing verbose and largely impenetrable memoranda on any number of subjects—for example, general education, academic planning, the restructuring of both the faculty and administration:

> First, I do not believe that general educational requirements as presently conceived possess the educational coherence and pedagogic effectiveness they ought to. Secondly, given the wide diversity of students coming to our College and the different levels of their preparedness, we cannot assume a common background against which indispensable intellectual strivings can be plotted. Lastly, in view of the wide divergence of perceptions as to the nature of the major and the corresponding vagueness surrounding the utility of electives, we cannot presume any collegewide educational cohesiveness holding our curriculum together.
>
> Beyond these demonstrable weaknesses in our educational strategy, moreover, something more basic precludes a consensus as to what constitutes acquaintance with the values and issues of an egalitarian society as we enter the last quarter of this century. A more active and dialectic approach must be adopted and I believe our College has exactly the needed resources to bring this about.[5]
>
> *STRATEGY*
>
> Conceptual considerations must precede practical considerations, formal requirements, and established practice for planning *not to be ad hoc and piecemeal.*

Through a comprehensive curricular review, we must scrutinize actual course offerings, the rationale of academic requirements, the faculty's instructional capabilities, and the students' educational needs.

The evaluative side of planning must proceed with conceptual expectations that are statable and relevant to our University's instruction. We must review the aims of each course; the course's contribution to the department's philosophy and to the school's overall requirements; and the benefits of the course to students.[6]

This unending flurry of pronouncements kept faculty, administrators, and staff busy meeting, debating, and responding. Some became engaged and agitated, particularly when Diamandopoulos raised the related subjects of "effective academic-executive arrangements," the "university-wide concerns...of the administration," and his "authority," which was often.[7] More often than not, his comments surrounding the issue of the scope of his power/authority inflamed the greatest passion. Still, since for the most part nothing much came of the bustle, it usually dissipated. In the end, it was passed off as mostly a harmless artifice often used by failed academics, both faculty and administrators, to bolster their self-esteem.

Diamandopoulos also spoke often and at length on many other topics, but said very little. (The number of faculty who found him tiresome did not begin to increase noticeably until 1980. He enjoyed the support of many in the student government until the 1981-82 academic year.) He continually referred to change, progress, and how much more he still needed to accomplish, while what he actually did to promote teaching, education, or academic life was hardly discernible.

Loggerheads

It must be remembered that academic administrators faced with shrinking budgets year after year are significantly more disadvantaged than those who are not. Even if inclined, they cannot make innovations. They must spend an inordinate amount of time staggering from one brush fire to another in an attempt to minimize an institution's losses. Moreover, having to say "no" more often than "yes" generally sows seeds of ill will. A good number of faculty are convinced that they are special, their wants are unquenchable, they are never happy hearing bad news, and their frustrations are invariably directed at academic administrators. Diamandopoulos found himself in this unenviable position in all of his years at Sonoma State. Time and again, his pride, inflated sense of self, and poor judgment exacerbated the problem.

Censure #1

At the beginning of the 1980-81 academic year, with the dismissal of tenured faculty looming as the result of the declining enrollments and reduced budget, Diamandopoulos insisted on hiring an additional administrative assistant, Carl Ledbetter, who had been a graduate student at Brandeis University when he had been dean there. Not coincidentally, Diamandopoulos had been engaged to Ledbetter's ex-wife, although the relationship had been broken off before Ledbetter arrived at Sonoma State the previous year as acting dean of academic planning, a job for which he was neither trained nor qualified.

In spite of the fact that a search committee had been appointed to screen candidates for what many faculty believed was an unnecessary and redundant management position, it was assumed that the entire exercise was a sham, that Diamandopoulos from the beginning was determined to select Ledbetter to become part of his inner circle. The Academic Senate, by a vote of 16-0, with 3 abstentions, initially urged the President not to fill the position and instead to use the money to help avoid faculty layoffs. This advice was ignored; Diamandopoulos was, in fact, openly contemptuous of those questioning these sorts of decisions; they did not understand "his prerogatives," they were "meddling."

Alleging "favoritism" and "cronyism," the Academic Senate next voted 22-6, with 3 abstentions, to censure Diamandopoulos. The resolution was unfocused and long (almost three single-spaced pages) and complex (eleven "whereas" and three "resolved" clauses). The chair of the Academic Senate accused Diamandopoulos of violating "the moral standards of academia." In one of several memoranda exchanged, Diamandopoulos "repudiated" and "rejected" the censure, and attributed it to "recent misunderstandings."[8] He was supported by Sonoma State's lay Advisory Board:

> After hearing the report given by you, and discussing the matter *in camera*, the Board was convinced that your judgment was correct and understood your dilemma [sic]. The Board unanimously concluded that after four [sic] years of public service to the University, you should be commended on your first-rate

performance in carrying out your job as mandated...and commended [for] your dedication to our common cause at Sonoma State University. The University expected and has received strong and able leadership from you and will accept nothing less.[9]

Prior to this endorsement of Diamandopoulos, this local council decided that it was unnecessary to invite representatives of the Academic Senate to present their views.

The students, showing a modicum of wisdom not exhibited by their elders, passed their own resolution calling "upon both the President and the Academic Senate to cease persuing [sic] personal vindication and make an honest and forthright effort to resolve the issues between them."[10]

The entire incident was much ado about very little. Its real significance is that it was indicative of the reservoir of enmity and distrust Diamandopoulos had built up in a relatively short period of three years. Unhappily, it was also a portent of things to come.

Censure #2

In the late spring of 1982, the Academic Senate voted, 17 to 3, again to censure Diamandopoulos. This time faculty were angry that he had unilaterally granted tenure to the acting vice president for academic affairs and the dean of humanities over the objections of their respective academic departments, while at the same time twenty-four colleagues with permanent appointments—about 10 percent of the teaching staff—had been notified that they would probably be terminated for reasons of financial exigency—or as Diamandopoulos put it, "because of lack of funds or lack of work."[11]

Faculty claimed that Diamandopoulos's actions were in violation of California law, that he was obligated to consult with them on such personnel matters, which he had failed to do. On this point they were wrong. Their advice or approval was not needed; he had gotten authorization from the chancellor's office before making his decision to grant tenure to the two, and he had the legal right to act as he did. Nonetheless, his timing was undeniably dreadful. What he had done greatly contributed to the acrimony on campus, and was again a reflection of how strained relationships were between Diamandopoulos and the faculty. Not unexpectedly, the chancellor of the university system and its Board of Trustees again sided with Diamandopoulos.

No Confidence

In an effort to further discredit Diamandopoulos after the censure, the Academic Senate unanimously agreed to conduct a referendum to determine the level of satisfaction across the campus with him and his administration. He had publicly made the claim that the Academic Senate did not represent the majority of the faculty, and the poll was proposed to ascertain whether this was the case. In addition, a number of faculty expressed the hope that the results of the survey could be used as the foundation for a vote of no confidence on Diamandopoulos that would at least force him to moderate some of his most extreme positions, the ones they found most harmful.

Of the slightly more than 70 percent of the eligible faculty who returned ballots, two-thirds expressed no confidence in Diamandopoulos. When asked to name the "most important single weakness" of Sonoma State, a significant number indicated that it was the administration, the President, or administration-faculty conflict. Overall, more than 70 percent of the respondents rated Diamandopoulos's leadership as poor; 50 percent labeled him incompetent. (In this inventory, only the University's food service was ranked lower than Diamandopoulos.)

A month after the referendum, officers of the Academic Senate asked Diamandopoulos to step down as President. As surely expected, he rejected this suggestion out of hand:

> I have no reason and no intention to resign. On the contrary, I intend to honor fully my commitment to Trustees, to the University, and to the public to assist in SSU's development as a leading center of learning. Although progress has been made in realizing that goal, much remains to be done.
>
> I find the support of the Trustees, the chancellor, discerning faculty, students, staff, and the public most heartening. With such collective support, I have no doubt that SSU will become a truly distinctive and distinguished institution of higher education.
>
> Now that your formal request has been made and denied, I consider the matter closed....[12]

Diamandopoulos did not believe that it was necessary to take steps to placate those nondiscerning faculty with whom he had been quarreling.

Censure #3: The Final Pratfall (at Sonoma)

In 1983, the Academic Senate at Sonoma State voted again to censure Diamandopoulos. This time faculty were unhappy over his failure
to consult them before greatly reducing the funding and threatening to
terminate a number of individuals in the office of student affairs. In
crippling this unit's effectiveness, the faculty was displeased that
Diamandopoulos had violated "the shared governance mechanisms
and practices of the University," and characterized his actions as "unprofessional behavior."

It was generally understood that under pressure from newly mandated cutbacks by the California State University System it was necessary for the administration to take immediate steps to offset an
impending budget deficit. The concern on the part of many faculty
was with "the process," often a mantra for faculty preparing for certain humiliation and defeat. The Academic Senate felt it had a duty to
uphold faculty rights in the face of Diamandopoulos's continuing ar-
bitrariness. Its leadership argued that by failing to consult faculty,
he had once again disregarded accepted campus tradition, and the
moral obligation to be fair and honest.

In its defense, the administration responded that the problem it was
dealing with was not a matter within the purview of faculty, but simply a managerial issue of how best to allocate limited resources. In
large part, the debate centered around the question of whether those
targeted for dismissal were or were not faculty members. Some in the
office of student affairs had long been considered as such at Sonoma;
the Diamandopoulos administration ignored this fact.

Diamandopoulos was convinced that the never-ending strife between his administration and the faculty was no more than a reflection
of more general escalating adversarial relationships at Sonoma engendered by the growing strength of collective bargaining on American
campuses. Whatever the reason for the mutual distrust, it would seem
that he was disliked by a larger proportion of those in his charge than
most of his counterparts elsewhere. It was apparent that many senior
faculty at Sonoma State were determined to monitor and, when possible, harass him, whatever the costs to them or to the School. As one
faculty leader put it, Diamandopoulos's continued failure to follow
established procedures "should not go unpunished." Faculty activists
were completely focused on forcing Diamandopoulos to embrace a

more democratic style. He was just as focused on resisting their efforts.

After 1980, a significant number of faculty had become fully convinced that Diamandopoulos was not truly committed to the widely accepted academic tradition of joint decision making, had grave misgivings about his motives and actions, had accordingly set upon a campaign to expose and embarrass him, and hoped in the end to prompt his resignation. On very few campuses does one find faculty as angered and unrelenting; not many college or university presidents are embroiled in such public and endless conflict with faculty. An even smaller number of academic administrators seem to be as combative and to so thoroughly enjoy being the source and center of controversy as much as Diamandopoulos did. It provided him with another opportunity to draft a memorandum. Fighting did not bother him; it was only losing that did. He was convinced that compromise would weaken his authority. He would not budge.

This time the censure—and more importantly Sonoma's lingering unrest and unfavorable publicity in the wider academic world for having fired tenured faculty—prompted a response which offered the promise that faculty complaints might at last be taken seriously, investigated, and perhaps addressed. The incoming chancellor of the California State University System requested that the faculty outline four disputed areas which they most wanted resolved. In their petition, the faculty stated that they were most concerned with the "prolonged and destructive conflict" on the Sonoma State campus during much of Diamandopoulos's tenure as President.

In the summer of 1983, a five-member panel was named by the chancellor's office to look into the multifaceted charges against Diamandopoulos. After the inquiry, there was a confidential report which was characterized by some Trustees "as so negative that it would have to be rejected or Diamandopoulos would have to be discharged." The Board soon met in an over four-hour closed-door meeting, after which Diamandopoulos was told that he had lost the support both of the majority of the Trustees (one of whom, according to press reports, he called "a Jewish bitch") and the chancellor. He was given the option to resign, which he immediately, very publicly, and tearfully did.

A year and a half after nearly single-handedly polarizing the Sonoma State campus, he was hired by the Board of Trustees of Adelphi. In announcing the appointment, the chair of the Adelphi Board—who incidentally was chairman of the New York Stock Exchange—praised Diamandopoulos as "a leader; a man of action who can penetrate to the heart of an issue and chart a course of action."[13] This was surely a curious take on Diamandopoulos's administrative ability. Not many who were familiar with his error-prone years at Sonoma State would characterize him this way. He had done little else but distract faculty from their teaching and generate considerable divisiveness while there. Due in part to him, the school was a less effective educational institution in 1983 than in 1977.

It is not uncommon for Major League Baseball managers, National Basketball Association coaches, and National Football League coaches who, because of lapses in judgment or an inability to make the best use of personnel, lose games more often than they should, to be fired by one team and to be inexplicably rehired by another.[14] Still, it is hard to imagine that one with Diamandopoulos's record of muddle and penchant for fostering disharmony would be so fortunate.

That the Adelphi Board overlooked Diamandopoulos's damaging quirks and hired him would seem to call into question a system which gives lay boards this power. Given what was known about his tenure at Sonoma State, the 1985 Board of Trustees of Adelphi showed exceedingly poor judgment in choosing a proven failure to be the University's chief academic officer. It badly underestimated the strife and antagonism that would result from his appointment. It is unlikely its credulity is that unusual; there is nothing particularly special about these Trustees. Other lay academic governing boards in good faith surely also make decisions that are just as poor—and which also have unhappy results for colleges and universities.[15]

Financial Management at Adelphi

The most commonly heard justification for lay governing boards is the sound financial management they putatively provide colleges and universities. Since a smaller proportion of institutions of higher learning go bankrupt than bookstores or taverns, this assertion has, for the most part, gone unexamined. It would seem that skyrocketing tuition and the continuous growth of useless bureaucracy would prompt someone to consider the validity of this claim. It might be that there is ample evidence to show that the resources of colleges and universities are not being put to the best use. The financial picture at Adelphi in recent years hardly supports the belief that a governing board necessarily provides sound financial management to the college or university in its charge.

According to figures of the U.S. Department of Commerce's Integrated Postsecondary Education Data System (IPEDS) collected for the Department of Education, Adelphi University's revenues increased from $66.48 million in 1987 to $88.76 million in 1994. In 1987, 77.5 percent of this total came from student tuition and fees. In 1994, 82.7 percent came from these sources. Other institutions similar to Adelphi in other ways derive between 50 and 55 percent of nonappropriated revenues from tuition and fees; Adelphi's significantly larger number attests to how precarious its finances had become, and how necessary it was to spend and invest with care. The Adelphi Board was not judicious in this regard.

Moreover, 48.9 percent of Adelphi's expenditures went to instruction in 1987, while only 45.0 percent went to instruction in 1994. Paradoxically, over the eight years, a smaller proportion of the University's funds was being spent to educate students, but the University had become more dependent to sustain itself on what they paid in tuition and fees.

Endowment

One useful indicator of an institution of higher learning's financial health over time is its endowment, to which the governing board attends. A decreasing endowment is inauspicious, immediately suggesting that an institution's budget is out of balance or that its investments are not doing well. Perhaps there has not been prudent oversight of its resources. As table 5.1 shows, during the years of Peter Diamandopoulos's presidency of Adelphi, the school's endowment grew by between 60 and 65 percent, certainly not a figure that, on the face of it, would suggest poor management. Adelphi ranked in the thirty-fifth percentile "for schools of its class, among which endowments averaged $55,566,323."[16]

The numbers in table 5.1 are to some extent deceptive. It was not necessarily actions by the Board nor the administration of Adelphi that primarily accounted for the growth of its endowment. Most of the increase can be attributed to the ordinary appreciation of most investments during this eleven-year period. When Diamandopoulos became

TABLE 5.1
Adelphi University, Market Value of Endowment, 1985-1995 (in Thousands)

Year	Endowment* Beginning of Year	Endowment* End of Year
1985		5,900
1986	5,900	
1988		5,448
1989	5,448	
1991		6,521
1992	6,521	
1994		9,644
1995	9,660	

* Market value dollars.

Source: casper.nsf.gov.

President of Adelphi the broad equity market in the United States was just beginning a steep ascent. For example, the Dow-Jones Industrial Average was between 1500 and 1600 at the end of 1985 (closing at 1546.67 on December 31). At the end of 1989, even after the collapse of the American junk-bond market, it was not far from 2800. In the early winter of 1995, it had passed 5000.

Adelphi's endowment yield which was 2.8 percent in 1985 and 3.2 percent in 1986 had fallen to 1.1 percent by 1995. This 1995 figure ranked Adelphi in the seventh percentile among schools of its class, which earned an average yield of 4.9 percent for the year.[17] Neither the figure of 1.1 nor 4.9 is impressive. A competent professional investment firm could have earned this rate of return. It is unclear what a governing board, even with a number of individuals with business experience, could add. Those in business also depend on professional investment firms to manage their resources.

Against the overall financial picture in the United States, the figures in tables 5.1 and 5.2, taken together, would suggest that governing boards are hardly necessary (or useful) for overseeing the investments of a college or university. Table 5.2 shows the changes in endowment of fourteen New York colleges and universities with limited assets between 1985 and 1995. Since most outperformed Adelphi's growth in endowment, its increase here was not in any way exceptional, in spite of what Board members repeatedly attested. It was, in fact, less than adequate. At the same time, the returns of half of the schools in table 5.2 are also not particularly striking.

TABLE 5.2
Endowments*, 14 New York Colleges and Universities,
1985-1995 (in Thousands)

Institution	Endowment, 1985	Endowment, 1995	Percent Increase
Adelphi	5,900	10,759	82
Alfred	16,199	36,997	128
Clarkson	24,375	72,559	198
C. of New Rochelle	4,157	8,793	112
Elmira	12,659	13,798	9
Hobart/Wm. Smith	19,919	52,663	164
Hofstra	20,598	60,713	195
Houghton	4,619	9,654	109
Iona	6,389	10,378	62
Marist	2,446	6,432	163
Mercy	4,794	10,444	118
Polytechnic	12,085	17,483	45
St. Bonaventure	9,344	8,056	-14
St. Francis	8,528	14,670	72

* End of year market value dollars.

Source: casper.nsf.gov.

Of the thirteen other colleges and universities in table 5.2, eight had larger percentage increases in their endowment between 1985 and 1995 than Adelphi. It is noteworthy that two of the five which did not, Elmira College and St. Bonaventure University, were the subject of considerable attention in the larger academic community during the period as a result of questionable behavior on the part of their administrations.[18]

Attracting Funds

As is apparent from table 5.3, the Adelphi Board and President Diamandopoulos did not have much success attracting contributions which might be used to increase the school's endowment. The $8.7 million in gifts to Adelphi over the eleven years of Diamandopoulos's presidency—not an impressive amount in itself —barely covered his costs to the University in salary, benefits, and expenses over that period.

TABLE 5.3
Private Gifts, Unrestricted, Adelphi University, 1985-1995

Year	Amount in Dollars
1985	396,088
1986	1,298,213
1987	1,064,521
1988	645,984
1989	524,512
1990	668,975
1991	522,713
1992	462,996
1993	1,094,763
1994	954,804
1995	1,090,802

Source: Exhibit, P-94.

Trustee Giving

The Board's minutes show that Trustees were constantly exhorted to support Adelphi financially. On February 27, 1987, they were reminded that "66 percent of the Trustees have contributed a total of $217,000 this year." However: "Mr. Byrne emphasized the need for 100 percent Board participation." On May 11, 1988, they were again told that "Trustee participation is an integral part of the fundraising enterprise and is an area that needs to be strengthened." The March 7, 1990 Board minutes state that "members were urged to become more active in the area of fundraising." Later that year "Mr. Carlino requested of Dr. Diamandopoulos a list of Trustee annual commitments apropos of development efforts, for he will contact each member regarding this issue."

Some Trustees still resisted becoming part of the "team in terms of raising money," and, as a result, the pleas and pressure continued. At the meeting on December 7, 1994, they were reminded both at the beginning and at the end that "it is imperative that Trustee participation be involved with giving. Therefore, the President, Peter Goulandris, and I [the chair] will see each of you, personally, to discuss your long- and short-term commitments."

The Board as a whole did not meet its responsibility last year as far as contributions were concerned. Mr. Goulandris wrote to Trustees [and] received some responses, but no additional contributions. We must do better. Mr. Goulandris, Mrs. Procope, and the President will be visiting individual Trustees and asking specific advice on fundraising.

The appeals continued at a number of Board meetings in 1995 and 1996. On March 8, 1995, Peter Goulandris[19] again implored his colleagues:

As Trustees of Adelphi, we have answered the President's call and have come to his side with strong moral support and much wise counsel. Until now—with a few exceptions—we have not come forward with the financial support that is now needed to show the seriousness and commitment which is necessary to engage other people, foundations, and organizations of substance.

Our confidence and dedication in making the President's dream a reality is now put to the test and we must and will meet the challenge. I will lead the way with a substantial commitment and I will discuss this commitment and get commitments from those members of the Board most capable of providing financial support. After we meet the core group, Mrs. Procope and I will discuss with each of you what we have accomplished and then ask for your pledge....

The Basis of Evaluation—and High Praise

This focus by the Trustees on their own philanthropy was in the larger framework of their overriding concern with Adelphi's financial affairs—the precarious state of its finances, its budget, its investments, capital improvements, costs, audits, and the like. Policies and procedures surrounding these matters are what engaged them most. They never doubted or looked beyond Diamandopoulos's reports of his many accomplishments. He understood and spoke their language when he told them that the books were balanced; they approved when they saw that the campus was in good repair. They were fulsome in praising his accomplishments in these matters; these were the standards by which he was primarily measured. With regularity, they expressed their unreserved satisfaction at Board of Trustees meetings. The following excerpts are from the meeting of November 14, 1986.

Mr. Lovely presented the report of the Finance Committee. He complimented Dr. Diamandopoulos and Ms. Bernabeu for the comprehensive report that was mailed to everyone.

Mr. McMillan commended Dr. Diamandopoulos and Ms. Bernabeu for their business-like financial report.

Mr. Wydler commended Dr. Diamandopoulos for the courage he showed in closing the costly para-academic programs.

Mr. Conklin complimented the President on the improved appearance of the campus.

There is little doubt of what the interests and priorities of the Trustees were.

The solid support the Board gave the President over the years was in large part due to its being convinced that he was realistic and pragmatic, (neither of which proved to be true). As time passed, the abiding faith increased to adulation. Here are some excerpts from the Board chair's comments at the September 22, 1993 meeting.

With all the flux and turmoil in higher education, we are fortunate that Adelphi University is today a beacon of hope and stability. This has been achieved largely through the brilliant conceptualization of what a modern, first-rate university of the future must be by our President, Peter Diamandopoulos.

Dr. "D" is a visionary, a Renaissance man who is dedicated to setting a positive example for higher education in this country and in the democratic nations of the world....

In a world where we see a lack of moral courage and a void in intellectual leadership, Dr. "D" stands out....

With the tenacity of a bulldog he holds on and keeps pushing....

Dr. "D's" dreams and vision of creating the most distinguished national educational institution are coming to fruition with each passing day....

Due to his global outlook and orientation, he realized long before others what the United States needed to compete in the new worldwide marketplace....

It is, indeed, a distinct honor and pleasure for me to chair this Board of outstanding individuals and leaders from various sectors of our community and to work to help Dr. "D" achieve his dream for Adelphi....

Diamandopoulos often reciprocated, eulogizing the Board. It would be difficult to remain on the Adelphi Board and not venerate Diamandopoulos and one's colleagues for their wisdom, goodness, and other virtues.[20]

Most members of the Board did not appear to have the capacity or another reference point to take Diamandopoulos's full measure as an academic administrator. For the most part, all that they used to evaluate his effectiveness was what he told them about his plans, and his and their successes. In 1990, he told a magazine reporter about "a master construction plan to spend $250 million in phases during the 1990s to replace and modernize some of the 21 buildings on campus."

> "First we'll build dormitories," says Diamandopoulos, "with beds for 3,000 students" (Adelphi now is able to house 1,100 students). "An academic center will be built next, with large conference rooms to create a condition of collegiality and induce academic discourses." This will be followed by construction of an amphitheater and then a chapel, all by 1996, the University's 100th anniversary. During later phases of construction, a student activity center would be built, along with a 1,000-car parking garage.[21]

According to the minutes, at the June 20, 1990 Board meeting, "Dr. Diamandopoulos outlined the accomplishments achieved at the University during the past year.... 'We are imparting distinction and character to the University to attract high quality students and grants from funding agencies.'"

What the Trustees were told was self-congratulatory—positive, flattering, and pleasing, although mostly untrue. At the March 7, 1990 Board meeting when they heard the exaggerations that "we are attracting the kinds of students we want in relation to our long-term goals" and "student applications are up and the quality of student we are attracting is improving," they simply took this at face value. Why should they believe otherwise? Diamandopoulos seemed capable of working miracles. Besides, they did not know (or did not seem to know or did not want to know) of a way to determine what was valid and what was a distortion, and how central the question of the recruitment of students was to the future of Adelphi. It was enough to hear repeated assurances.

As it turned out, facts often did not support claims. It can readily be shown that the Trustees were deliberately misled. This is best done by reviewing in chapter 6 Diamandopoulos's eleven-year record at Adelphi. The performance of the Adelphi Board of Trustees cannot really be judged without judging the performance of Diamandopoulos. He failed because it failed first. It failed because of the institution of lay governing boards.

In hindsight, the missteps and their consequences enumerated in chapter 6 seem almost inevitable.

Notes

1. See chapter 4, note 5.
2. When asked about the decision on three occasions in the spring of 1999 ("What was it about Diamandopoulos that prompted you and your colleagues to select him?;" "Why did the Board choose Diamandopoulos and not someone else?;" "How was the decision to hire Diamandopoulos made?"), the chair of the search committee was at once vague, defensive, apologetic, and unhelpful. He twice said that the Board was looking for a "forceful leader." "He came across as very strong, articulate, and scholarly," he told a widely circulated magazine. (Curtis Rist, with Ron Arias and Amalia Duarte, "For Its President, Little Adelphi U. Is a Place of Higher Earning," *People,* 13 November, 1995, p. 174). In a lengthy discussion with him which focused exclusively on this matter, the chair—who at an earlier time had been chair of the Adelphi Board—added that people spoke well of Diamandopoulos, but he could not recall who these individuals were or what they had said. He was not able to find and provide me with any records, i.e., letters of recommendation or committee meeting minutes, of the search. Four different faculty members confided that the Board knew a great deal about Diamandopoulos's contempt for faculty, and that the decision was made, in the words of one, "to inflict pain." Another surmised: "It resented that we were unionized and united, and planned to use him to control us." Although not implausible, they could offer no evidence to support these conjectures.
3. See, for example, Warren Bennis, *The Leaning Ivory Tower,* San Francisco, CA: Jossey-Bass, 1973. Describing one interview for the presidency of Northwestern University with "the chairman of the search committee, who was also a Northwestern trustee and chairman of the board of Harris Trust Company in Chicago; the associate dean of Northwestern's school of speech and drama, representing the faculty; and the president of the Northwestern student association," Bennis writes: "I *liked* them, particularly the student, who asked the most penetrating and direct questions. The faculty representative appeared to be gentle and perceptive and a remarkable listener. The chairman was the least relaxed and sometimes irrelevant, going off on a tack of his own which I couldn't always understand." (p. 24).
4. A dozen years after Diamandopoulos became President, it was reported in one newspaper that "the University Trustees thought Adelphi had to do something radical to survive in the increasingly competitive world of small, regional liberal arts colleges. And so they hired Dr. Diamandopoulos, who argued that Adelphi could be saved only by raising its intellectual sights and discontinuing or cutting back lesser programs." (William H. Honan, "Adelphi, a Little University with Big Ideas" [print edition], or "At Adelphi, Crash Course in Major Thinking" [electronic version], *New York Times,* 5 February, 1997, p. B1). The source and validity of this statement are unknown.

   The first paragraph of the Adelphi press release announcing Diamandopoulos's appointment as President, refers to his "reputation for strong fiscal management and high intellectual standards" ("Dr. Peter Diamandopoulos Named President of Adelphi University," Adelphi University News Service, 1985). In an open letter welcoming Diamandopoulos to the Adelphi campus, the chair of the Board of Trustees wrote: "We believe that his qualifications are 'right' for Adelphi at this point of its history" (Letter from John J. Phelan, Jr. to Dear Friends of Adelphi, 28 June, 1985).

5. Memorandum from Dr. Peter Diamandopoulos to Dr. Ellen Amsterdam, 16 May, 1978.
6. Memorandum from Peter Diamandopoulos to Sonoma State University Faculty, 9 October, 1979.
7. Diamandopoulos was relentless in his efforts to reorganize the campus so that the lines of authority were clear, so that everyone understood that he—Peter Diamandopoulos—was in charge. It appeared that he wanted to convince himself as much as others of this. He obsessively wrote on this subject:

> At the same time, I will never yield the executive prerogatives delegated to me by the Board of Trustees and designed to make possible effective academic leadership of the School. Implicit and explicit in such leadership is responsibility for the welfare of the University in all its several aspects—including (as I have stated on numerous occasions), but not exhausted by, the interests of the faculty. (Memorandum from Peter Diamandopoulos to Dr. Mildred Dickemann, 18 September, 1980).

As a matter of course, faculty do not like hearing such truths, which more often than not creates considerable resentment.
8. Memorandum from Peter Diamandopoulos to the Campus Community, 17 October, 1980.
9. Letter from Lois A. Prentice, chairperson, Sonoma State University Advisory Board to Dr. Diamandopoulos, 20 October, 1980.
10. Memorandum from the Associated Students to the Campus Community, (stamped: "received") 29 October, 1980.
11. Believing that President Diamandopoulos had violated widely accepted academic principles, a number of the affected faculty members appealed to the American Association of University Professors for assistance. Following its usual practice, the Association sent an investigating team to the Sonoma State campus. As background to its inquiry, the committee noted: "Other component institutions of the California State University have also faced problems with enrollment during the past few years, but, with a single and limited exception at California State College, Bakersfield, they have managed to avoid terminating the appointment of any tenured faculty member."

After completing its investigation, the team submitted a lengthy report in which it concluded that the Sonoma State administration had not demonstrated that financial conditions warranted firing so many individuals. It found sufficient evidence that the "administration, by proceeding essentially unilaterally to decide which faculty appointments were to be terminated and by not providing faculty members with an opportunity to be heard before the termination of their appointments became effective, denied those faculty members the safeguards of academic due process...."

The last paragraph of the report was the most damning to Diamandopoulos, and decidedly put to rest any question of whether or not he was qualified to hold power—not so much whether or not at times others believed that he was a dissembler, but whether he was so devious and unprincipled that he was completely unqualified for any position of trust:

> Instances of abuse by the administration of institutional standards and procedures so as to assure the retention of favored faculty members while causing

the release of others, particularly through its manipulation of Teaching Service Areas [i.e., courses which faculty were qualified to teach], have dampened the climate for academic freedom at Sonoma State University, leaving much of the faculty alienated and mistrustful.

Quite simply, by cashiering his critics and working to keep his allies on the faculty, Diamandopoulos had disqualified himself to give or carry out orders in an institution of higher learning. Diamandopoulos is certainly not the first academic administrator found to have behaved dishonorably. It is not often, however, that such a detailed pattern of treachery is uncovered, documented, and published. (A careful search by the Adelphi Board, or a competent professional hired to find acceptable presidential candidates, would surely have discovered this publication.)

As promised, Diamandopoulos had made Sonoma State unique; as a result of his capriciousness, his administration was censured by the American Association of University Professors, a decision taken only occasionally. (See "Academic Freedom and Tenure: Sonoma State University [California]," *Academe,* Volume 69, Number 3, May/June 1983, pp. 3-12).

12. Memorandum from Peter Diamandopoulos to Dr. Barry Godolphin, 24 June, 1982. Diamandopoulos's dismissive and arrogant "I consider the matter closed" will undoubtedly remind some of Shakespeare's Richard III's amusing retort when confronted with a screed of his murderous deeds: "Harp not on that string."

13. Quoted in Gaye LeBaron, "Insight," *Press Democrat* (Santa Rosa, California), 5 June, 1985.

14. One such individual that comes readily to mind is the basketball coach Don Nelson. After presiding over the decline of the Golden State Warriors, he briefly coached the New York Knicks with similar results, and is presently (in 1998-99) coaching the Dallas Mavericks.

15. One five-year study of the presidency at thirty-two colleges and universities identified one-quarter as failures. (Robert Birnbaum, *How Academic Leadership Works: Understanding Success and Failure in the College Presidency,* San Francisco, CA: Jossey-Bass, 1992, p. 195). This sizable figure suggests that at a minimum the criteria and the decision-making process used in selecting college and university presidents could be improved.

16. William B. Busa, editor, *Critical Comparisons of American Colleges & Universities,* MEMEX Press, 1997. (Source: IPEDS).

17. Ibid.

18. *See* "Report, College and University Government: Elmira College (New York)," *Academe,* Volume 79, Number 5, September/October 1993, pp. 42-52; and "Report, Academic Freedom and Tenure: St. Bonaventure University (New York)," *Academe,* Volume 81, Number 4, July/August 1995, pp. 65-73.

19. Goulandris, obviously, was one of a handful of Trustees who were quite generous toward Adelphi. According to summaries provided by the University, between 1986 and 1996, six Trustees or the companies or foundations with which they were associated made significant monetary contributions:

Trustee A: $56,600 between 1989 and 1992, and 1995.

Trustee B: $115,000 between 1990 and 1995.

Trustee C: $235,000 between 1993 and 1996.

Trustee D: $315,915 between 1988 and 1989, and 1992 and 1996.

Trustee E: $128,000 between 1987 and 1991, and 1993 and 1996.

Trustee F: $265,500 between 1986 and 1988, 1990, and 1995-1996.

The combined gifts of these six totaled $1,116,015. (Exhibits R-BBB, R-EEE, R-GGG, R-III, R-JJJ, R-KKK).

20. A content analysis of the minutes of a sample of twenty-four Board of Trustees meetings held between 1988 and 1995 found thirty instances of praise. In half, the President is being congratulated; in close to a third, the President is flattering Trustees. The most constant theme was a reaffirmation of loyalty and support. At the same time, the various problems facing Adelphi are given much less attention. For example, the steady decline in undergraduate enrollments (a matter given considerable attention in chapter 6) is mentioned only eleven times; more often than not it is glossed over, dismissed as a minor matter, due merely to "a dwindling pool." (This last observation was made after nearly a decade of the "scarcity of quality students.")

21. Christopher Elias, "University President Learns at the School of Hard Knocks," *Insight,* 12 March, 1990, p. 39.

6

The Diamandopoulos Years at Adelphi

Peter Diamandopoulos's reputation as provocative, confrontational, and intense preceded his arrival at Adelphi University in 1985. He relished the notoriety, convinced that these traits added to his luster as an effective, no-nonsense academic administrator, and would serve to enhance his success. He invited John Silber, the provocative, confrontational, and intense president of Boston University, to speak at his inauguration. The affair cost the University in excess of $100,000; self-important seems to be another adjective that would aptly describe Diamandopoulos.

In a long inaugural prelection, Diamandopoulos declared that Adelphi University "has the obligation to assert its own distinctive philosophy of academic purpose and to embark upon educating a new generation of leaders. I visualize our mission to be none other than nurturing the best intellect, firing the imagination, and preparing gifted minds because American higher education is so in doubt about its central mission." He asserted that the school would have to be "restructured, reoriented, and transformed." It would no longer do simply to provide vocational preparation to local students from blue-collar families. Adelphi would become world class by attracting its students from across America and abroad.[1]

This address was more than the usual platitudinous, ceremonial oratory. It was a declaration that Diamandopoulos was planning to lead the school on a new course: Adelphi would plunge into the Diamandopoulos era.

From the beginning, it was evident that Diamandopoulos intended to strengthen the liberal arts at Adelphi. He envisioned integrating the curricula of the professional schools with the arts and sciences. Rather then following the conventional mode of finding money to lure academic stars and fund highly visible research to improve academics, he believed that inspired faculty and strong administrative leadership would raise Adelphi's academic quality. In 1986, he summed up this strategy: "Then we can have both a better educational institution and also fund it better. The academics will pull in the money. Very unorthodox." One faculty supporter of his plan observed that "his ambitions in curriculum far exceed those of the faculty. He has a much more grandiose vision of what can and should be done. There may be a gap between what the facts are and what he thinks is realistic."[2] This proved to be prescient.

Diamandopoulos's first task after arriving at Adelphi was to stabilize its precarious finances. He appeared to be quite successful at this. He and his staff ended a long period of operating deficits; the budget was balanced for ten years between 1985 and 1995. At the same time, in large part by collecting overdue accounts, cash reserves and the endowment increased tenfold over the years—from $4 million to between $40 and $45 million. In addition, over $45 million was invested in deferred maintenance and other physical improvements. New telephone and computer systems and hardware were installed, classrooms, residence halls, and offices were refurbished, laboratories and the campus theater were modernized.

Diamandopoulos pressed forward with the agenda which he was convinced would turn Adelphi into a first-rate liberal arts college. To this end, he moved to reduce the faculty teaching load from four to three courses a semester. He envisioned some faculty members using the extra time to engage in research, which could enhance Adelphi's visibility and prestige, or to improve their teaching. (He surely did not foresee that so many would use the time to more vigorously pursue a campaign against him, with the goal of eventually bringing him down.) Diamandopoulos also worked to improve the quality of intellectual life on campus. He set about bringing in, mostly on a visiting basis, a handful of high profile faculty. A number of public intellectuals, a majority of whom were known for their conservative political and/or economic views, were invited to share their ideas with the campus community.

Moreover, along with promoting the core curriculum, Diamandopoulos pushed forward other initiatives. By 1995, he was instrumental in transforming the honors program into an Honors College that could accommodate up to 187 students, and in establishing the Society of Mentors, which makes use of selected faculty and administrators to be "intellectual role models" and sponsors for all freshmen and sophomores.

The Honors College, Diamandopoulos believed, would enable Adelphi to recruit a cadre of bright and ambitious undergraduates who would promote and elevate thought and creativity on campus. As described in University publications, the purpose of the Honors College was to use "a distinctive course of study" to educate exceptional and gifted students "for leadership." Honors College offerings, again utilizing a small number of handpicked faculty, were designed to prepare students "to speak and write effectively, to reason accurately, to recognize and express differences in quality between the grand and the mundane, the genuine and the specious." One special feature of the Honors College was its "American emphasis," with a number of classes in the humanities and social sciences focusing on the legacy of the Enlightenment from the past to the present.

To be admitted to the Honors College and be eligible for its generous scholarships, a student had to score at least 1200 (out of a possible 1600) points on the nationally administered Scholastic Aptitude Test, and in other ways show intellectual potential; to graduate, it would be necessary to write a senior thesis.

The primary responsibility of the approximately sixty administrators and faculty involved in the Society of Mentors was to bring about the "intellectual transformation" of all Adelphi students, giving particular attention to their "abilities, hopes, and potentials." A mentor was expected to be a great deal more than a mere academic advisor; a student could also expect a great deal more than a superficial relationship through meaningful conversations with a "trusted consultant" and "guide." The program's ultimate objective was to move students to become "intellectually empowered and informed."

As a result of these accomplishments—of his vision and what appeared to be his unrelenting efforts—Diamandopoulos was seen by his supporters as Adelphi's "savior." They were captivated by his old-world charm and what they took to be his unlimited erudition. He was a sage who could do no wrong. As one described it, he single-handedly turned around a school that was "in fiscal distress, physical disrepair, and curricular disarray" and "on the verge of collapse" when he became President. Some seemed to believe that the obvious and incessant feud between the President and the faculty was an accurate indicator of how well he was performing. Their loyalty was boundless.

The price for these gains, his critics countered, was much too high. To them, the University was in a free fall as a result of Diamandopoulos's programs and policies—and personal flaws. It was folly to believe that Adelphi could ever compete for students with Harvard or the University of Chicago, with Williams or Swarthmore. He was denounced as being nothing more than a mercurial megalomaniac, a petty despot, out of touch with reality. They pointed to several developments to make their case.

Enrollments

Most bothersome, even to some of Diamandopoulos's staunchest allies, was the continually declining number of students, most notably undergraduates, the majority of whom paid tuition and brought in much needed government dollars in financial aid to Adelphi. The recurring theme here was that the most educationally sound or best devised programs would be of little value if there were an insufficient number of students to support and benefit from them. As is evident from table 6.1, Adelphi's enrollments had dropped precipitously and dangerously during Diamandopoulos's tenure as President.

Between 1985 and 1996, the number of full-time undergraduates fell alarmingly from 4,658 to 2,205. With one exception, between fall 1989 and fall 1990, the annual decrease was uninterrupted. The administration's response to the growing crisis was initially to point to "demographics": the contention was that the pool of high school graduates was shrinking, and that this was a time when it was necessary for all colleges and universities, regardless of their quality or reputation, to tighten their belts.

In all, undergraduate enrollment fell by more than 50 percent. Since graduate and professional enrollments hardly declined, this tempered the decrease for the entire University.

If it were not for the 11 percent decrease in graduate and professional enrollments between 1995 and 1996, their numbers would have actually increased over the eleven-year period. Nonetheless, in 1985 they were only half of the undergraduate enrollment; by 1996, their numbers were nearly the same, although Diamandopoulos was convinced they were not essential to Adelphi's viability.

In any case, the steadily diminishing size of the student body, which totaled 37 percent over a decade, understandably attracted most everyone's attention; to most it was worrisome.

The steady downturn in enrollment was most noticeable in incoming freshmen, as clearly seen in table 6.2.

TABLE 6.1
Full-Time Equivalent Enrollments, Adelphi University, 1985-1996

Year	Undergraduates	Graduates*	Total for University
Fall 1985	4,658	2,326	6,984
Fall 1986	4,462	2,338	6,800
Fall 1987	4,253	2,141	6,394
Fall 1988	4,040	1,993	6,033
Fall 1989	3,768	1,919	5,687
Fall 1990	3,779	1,960	5,739
Fall 1991	3,644	2,354	5,998
Spring 1992	3,377	2,475	5,852
Fall 1992	3,293	2,589	5,882
Spring 1993	3,074	2,718	5,792
Fall 1993	3,047	2,688	5,735
Spring 1994	2,931	2,876	5,807
Fall 1994	2,984	2,646	5,630
Spring 1995	2,766	2,637	5,403
Fall 1995	2,560	2,448	5,008
Spring 1996	2,405	2,350	4,755
Fall 1996	2,205	2,171	4,376

* Graduate and professional enrollments.

Sources: 1985-1990, New York State Education Department, Bureau of Postsecondary Education Research and Information Systems/HEDS (07/11/1994); 1991-1996, Adelphi University Admissions Office "Fall 1996 Target Report YTD Summary."

TABLE 6.2
Adelphi University Freshmen Headcount, 1985-1996

Year	Number
1985	958
1986	856
1987	796
1988	799
1989	822
1990	850
1991	737
1992	588
1993	512
1994	568
1995	385
1996	311

Source: New York State Education Department.

In 1985, 958 freshmen matriculated, and by 1987, the number was 796, a drop of 17 percent in two years. There were particularly large decreases between 1991 and 1992, and between 1994 and 1995. In 1996, freshman enrollments reached a low of 311. Between 1985 and 1996, they had plunged a troubling 67.5 percent. After more than a decade of Diamandopoulos's leadership, it had become evident to all except a handful of true believers in the administration and on the Board of Trustees that, notwithstanding the brave talk, Adelphi was rapidly moving toward financial ruin.

The administration reported to the Board of Trustees in 1993 that there were four factors "affecting successful enrollment management." First, the Long Island economy was weak. As a result, cost and affordability had become "preeminent considerations" for students and their families. Second, there was a substantial decline in the number of secondary school graduates, locally and nationally. Third, as a consequence of these two facts, institutions of higher learning needed to "compete more intensively" for students. Fourth, in recent years, there had been notable changes in the course of studies undergraduates were interested in pursuing.

The Board was assured by the administration that "through detailed planning, the hiring and training of new staff, and the comprehensive implementation of new recruitment systems, we have established a proactive, assertive, sales oriented approach to the educational marketing of both Adelphi's educational philosophy and the academic programs illustrative of that philosophy."

When the mildest misgivings were expressed about the steady slide in student enrollments, they were allayed, as no truly awkward or difficult questions were ever asked (at least publicly) by Trustees on the subject.[3] Those Trustees who might have been most uneasy about the steady decline in enrollments were no longer on the Board.

Diamandopoulos's unabating optimism was also comforting. On December 7, 1994, he told the Trustees, "I, as President, declare myself the 'dean of admissions' and [will] deal with the recruitment problem as an urgent priority. Only then can I assure the Board that the quality and numbers of students that must be enrolled at Adelphi, if the University is to remain solvent, will be realized."

The Diamandopoulos administration and the Board were convinced that the revitalized curriculum would lure undergraduates eager to immerse themselves in the liberal arts. It is hardly surprising that even with financial incentives, very few were tempted. At the same time, the sort of pre-professional students Adelphi had traditionally served were feeling less welcome and began to come in smaller and smaller numbers.

The President and Board failed to recognize that, as the years passed, declining enrollments had become a major problem which not only needed immediate attention but also needed to be promptly reversed. Enrollments were spiraling down at a dangerous rate. It is a testament to the indomitability of faith and academic folly, that anyone the least bit familiar with American undergraduates would press forward with Diamandopoulos's chimera, believing it could succeed. To be sure, a massive infusion of millions of dollars could have afforded Diamandopoulos time to test the feasibility of his efforts to attract a sufficient number of students who were serious about liberal learning and the life of the mind. However, essentially all that was forthcoming from the wealthy society he courted and emulated were encouragement, praise, and license to continue his risky venture.

The large differences in the decrease in enrollments between, on the one hand, undergraduates and, on the other hand, graduate and professional students turn out to be somewhat ironic and merit an additional comment. Diamandopoulos was convinced that the latter were a drag on the School—or at least on what he hoped Adelphi would become—and that as a consequence the already modest graduate programs should be cut back, that eventually some should be eliminated.

The administration and the Board of Trustees had drafted a secret plan to begin reducing academic programs peripheral to a focused undergraduate liberal arts curriculum. In effect, Diamandopoulos had convinced the Board to dilute and marginalize almost all of the University's graduate work, some of its least tenuous and most reliable revenue producing programs. Those that were not clearly profitable would be closed sooner rather than later: "The School of Nursing, the School of Social Work, and [the] Derner [Institute of Advanced Psychological Studies] are neither academically essential to the University, indispensable to its mission, nor as constituted now fiscally viable." (As a first step, the master's programs in English, chemistry, and earth sciences were discontinued.) The document was not even shared with the deans of the affected schools. If it had been, someone might have been in a position to caution and convince the President or some Trustees that Adelphi was setting out on a path that would surely lead to bankruptcy.

When the contents of a draft copy became known to an already restless faculty, existing tensions on campus were heightened. Diamandopoulos had now managed to alienate a segment of the faculty, those in applied fields, least likely to become involved in parochial disputes. Since it was apparent what the future held for them and that they had little to lose, their support eroded and they eventually joined forces with the dissidents from the Faculty Senate and the union.

Time was on the faculty's side; like Adelphi's student body, the number of Diamandopoulos's partisans among the faculty shrank year by year. Although those who challenged his authority were somewhat inept, they were, if nothing else, dogged. The majority saw Diamandopoulos running the school into the ground, and they cared. He was neither politically astute enough nor intellectually nimble enough to deal with the growing insurrection. Being no more clever or unerring in his judgment than his opponents, but falsely believing that he was, put Diamandopoulos at a distinct disadvantage. He was in over his head; again reality was beginning to overtake him. His polish and showmanship had taken him as far as they could. He would surely continue to make mistakes on which his adversaries could capitalize. As the pressure increased, he, in fact, went well beyond their expectations.

Not unlike numerous academic administrators across the country, Diamandopoulos comported himself like an effective chief executive officer and talked assuredly about matters being under control. At the same time, he could no longer ignore the many voices questioning his competence. This was a constant that he would have to endure. After 1991, his opponents became noisier and more shrill; stories about Adelphi's troubles were reaching beyond the Garden City community.

For its part, the Board of Trustees remained almost completely unfazed as if under a spell. It took at face value what Diamandopoulos told it; it did not look closely at the record. It remained convinced that whatever small adjustments might be necessary to better the University would surely catch Diamandopoulos's eye, that he would effectively handle matters.

Diamandopoulos had accomplished little in increasing Adelphi's endowment. This can be seen most clearly in the figures in table 6.3.

TABLE 6.3
Endowment Fund Raising, Adelphi University, 1985-1995*

Year Ending August 31	Money Added from Private Gifts and Grants
1985	$ 37,225
1986	$1,042,948
1987	$ 368,946
1988	$ 744,117
1989	$ 63,482
1990	$ 30,560
1991	$ 79,586
1992	$ 33,396
1993	$ 182,742
1994	$ 114,620
1995	$ 122,453
Total	$2,820,075

* Exhibit: P-164.

These figures need little explanation. In the eleven years of the Diamandopoulos administration, Adelphi University received less than $3 million in bequests to add to its endowment. The remainder of its growth was from transfers from the operating budget, capital gains, and interest and dividends from its portfolio. There was considerable talk of Diamandopoulos's prowess as a fundraiser, but the facts do not bear this out; the truth seems to be contrary to this fiction. Over the years, he spent a good deal of time and University money jetting first-class to Europe with his wife searching for benefactors, but to no avail.

Putting Adelphi on a sounder economic footing was a constant concern of the Board of Trustees. At its meeting on June 20, 1990, it was announced that "in light of the fact that previous attempts in this area [of soliciting money] have been unsuccessful,...a group of members of the management team and the staff will assume development duties that complement each of their current assignments. Public relations, community affairs, and cultural affairs personnel will work under the direct supervision of the President who will be taking a more direct and visible role in fundraising."

To inaugurate this initiative, a resolution was unanimously passed, which, in part, read:

WHEREAS, it is deemed in the best interest of Adelphi University to provide such expanded facilities in the City of New York in order to enable the Presi-

dent to achieve the University's development goals and thus assist him to
realize the proposed five-year plan [of his additional development duties];

RESOLVED, that the President is hereby asked on behalf of the University to
enter into a lease arrangement for suitable residential quarters in the City of
New York.

The cost of the first two-year lease of an "ancillary residence [for]
the President to assist him in his development activities" was $7,500 a
month. In part to save the $90,000 a year on rent, the Board next made
the decision to purchase a Manhattan apartment for $1.15 million,
ostensibly to enable the President to more efficiently conduct University business "in the City of New York." Indeed, Diamandopoulos's
fundraising activities were actually weakening, not strengthening,
Adelphi's economic fortunes. The Board remained steadfast in its
faith.

Diamandopoulos eventually acknowledged his lack of success at
fundraising, but denied that this was something he should be doing.
To the contrary, he expressed the belief that this was something he
should not necessarily be doing, that it was enough for him to be a
wellspring of ideas: "I don't think it is one of my responsibilities. Lots
of presidents don't raise a penny."[4]

With a limited endowment that had slowly appreciated (in part
because of modest investment returns) to between $6 and $7 million
by the mid-1990s, there was some question of how long Adelphi
could withstand the continuous erosion of its student body. Classes
were being taught and students were graduating, but in a number of
ways Adelphi was administratively in a shambles.

Diamandopoulos and the Board adamantly denied that anything
was wrong. At the same time, the administration was using stopgap
measures to address some of the most obvious and pressing problems.

Disenchantment and Strife

Needless to say, little of what the Adelphi administration did was to
the liking of most faculty. Even some in the administration grew
disenchanted. Between 1987 and 1995, the College of Arts and Sciences had five deans (two were acting and none lasted more than two
years), as did the School of Management and Business; the School of
Social Work and the School of Nursing each had three deans; there

were four directors of admissions.[5] Between 1992 and 1995, there were a half dozen changes in the provost's office.[6] Between 1987 and 1995, five individuals tried their hand as vice president of development, charged with fundraising,[7] and fifteen worked in various capacities as assistants to the President.[8] President Diamandopoulos's problem keeping the University's leadership in place was evident. Critics argued that this represented extraordinary turnover; supporters argued that Diamandopoulos was a perfectionist constantly in search of first-rate administrative talent.

As his circle of trusted advisers grew smaller, Diamandopoulos rejected any suggestion that this was, or might become, a matter about which he should be concerned. He repeatedly expressed the conviction that steady and great progress was being made at Adelphi, that what he had set out to accomplish was being realized.

Those who kept the faith adopted a siege mentality. Not only did Diamandopoulos isolate himself from the faculty, but after successfully establishing the policy isolating the Board from the faculty, he could more effectively convince Trustees that all was well.

The Erosion of Civility

The distrust between faculty and administration at Adelphi grew almost daily. Relationships were so bitter that, even when it was essential that both parties work together, there was confrontation, not accommodation. An excerpt from the minutes of a faculty meeting on February 27, 1995 exemplifies how agitated each side had become.

> L. Sullivan: I speak to the whole [administrative modified academic] plan [MAP or AP]—the process hurts me. To say we haven't responded! When we weren't asked to develop! There are assumptions underlying the AP which are wrong for Adelphi, destroying programs which make money and building up programs which cost us money. Should have been done from the bottom up, and the faculty would be very cooperative. We heard of alumni liaisons, which were then canceled. Faculty should have been involved from the early stages, then, we'd have a plan with goals you and we share and which would work.

> Dr. D: Faculty has a long history of not getting involved. No one is preventing any group from making an alternative plan—but administration can't wait through interminable discussions while pressures and events mount. The AP begins a strategy to address our crisis, and is a good start because it doesn't evade quantitative enrollment goals and qualitative academic improvements. The plan is adopted in principle by the Board (not line by line), [and] is reflective of the ongoing study of how the University fares.

P. Costello [acting dean]: Issues of arts and sciences in the MAP have been under discussion for more than three years. Divisional structure was discussed when I co-chaired a joint planning committee, and the provost's office unanimously endorsed this. Faculty who speak are those who don't approve. We don't need the approval of Professor P. Kelly, Professor L. Sullivan, Professor R. Axelrod, Professor S. Goldberg, Professor S. Windwer. The faculty has diverse opinions. The chairs of the arts voted, e.g., voted unanimously to create a center for the arts. It's not a matter of arriving at consensus, but of arriving at a plan.

T. Heffernan: If you are tired from hearing from single faculty, why haven't you called a faculty meeting of arts and sciences faculty?

P. Costello: In my twenty years as a faculty member, I have attended virtually every faculty meeting, and these seldom accomplished their stated goals. Usually they were attacks on initiatives. The college can operate as a whole or at the level of departments where it has a certain vitality and where substantive issues may be addressed. The college as a whole never discusses these as needed, and faculty have little in common beyond University politics. If one is interested in substantive issues and their discussion, then divisional faculty meetings are needed, where those in the division share points in common. To begin to address the real problems, we need to create a divisional structure.

T. Heffernan: The idea that College of Arts and Sciences faculty meetings are ineffective whereas divisional meetings would be effective, is, in technical terms, bullshit.

Dr. D: You are out of order, Professor Heffernan.

T. Heffernan: You'll be out of order if this goes on.

Dr. D: This is no place for personal disagreements with the dean.

(Several): I move to overrule the chair.

Dr. D: You are out of order.

D. Newton: Do we have a quorum?

S. Goldberg: There is a motion on the floor.

L. Sullivan: Request the parliamentarian to rule on the motion.

L Landesberg: [as parliamentarian] A motion to overrule the chair is always in order.

Dr. D.: Read your *Robert's Rules of Order* more carefully.

(Several): Motion to adjourn.

(Several): Seconded.

(Majority) Yes—(Minority) No.   PASSED.

VOTE: Faculty voted by leaving the meeting.

One need read but a small portion of this transcript to sense the great divide at Adelphi. The Adelphi Board of Trustees had provided Diamandopoulos another opportunity to polarize yet another campus. Given the constant tension, the outcome of this open meeting of closed minds was inevitable. The only uncertainty was how rapid the deterioration would be. The formal effort of faculty and administration to discuss and perhaps reach a compromise and agreement on some elements of a necessary academic plan for the near term to deal with student recruitment lacked good will on both sides, and was doomed from the start. As was the case at Sonoma State University, administrators talked past faculty; faculty talked past administrators. Administrators were talking to other administrators; faculty were talking to other faculty. When administrators and faculty got together, the minutes read like a script from a Marx Brothers slapstick, without the delightful presence of Margaret Dumont or Thelma Todd.

At a Faculty Senate meeting the same afternoon, President Diamandopoulos and Acting Dean Costello were accused of lying. The administration chose not to send a representative to attempt to defend itself, explain, make peace, or re-establish a dialogue with the faculty. Perceptions remained very much distorted.

There is no indication that any member of the Board of Trustees made an effort to fulfill one of its secondary responsibilities and intervene, to soothe the waters—and egos. This may well be because the Board was not kept fully abreast of how the many fundamental problems facing Adelphi, not only student recruitment, were being addressed. For example, in response to declining enrollments, on June 21, 1995, the senior vice president sent a memorandum to all of the deans that set forth a plan that would significantly change the delivery of instruction at Adelphi. He warned that "to be viable at 5000 FTES [full-time equivalent students], each member of the faculty must teach an *average* of 95 students each semester."

This means:

a student-faculty ratio of 17:1;

an increase in average lecture size from 22 to 32;

a reduction of faculty from FTEF [full-time equivalent faculty] 415 to FTEF 300;

> a reduction of lecture sections from 1,800 per year to 1,300 per year;
>
> and a change in workload to accommodate the fact that FTEF [of] 100+ now teach in non-lecture classes or sections....
>
> Therefore, we need radically to rethink both *the number and the nature* of our baccalaureate majors, to emphasize in the richest and most imaginative way the educational fundamentals. One way to do so, and to meet a number of other targets as well, is to reconceive our programs on the basis of courses rather than credits, so that students would take 32 to 36 courses to graduate, rather than 120 credits. (A course would not differentiate between lecture and lab, etc.)

While all of this would have entailed significant and complicated changes at Adelphi, it is not clear whether the Board was ever apprised of this plan.

> James T. Byrne, Jr.:
>
> Q: I was going to ask you whether or not it [the memorandum] was ever furnished to the Board of Trustees?
>
> A: Is this all attached, this whole thing?
>
> Q: Yes, the whole thing was one memo.
>
> Q[from Regent]: The first question, Mr. Byrne, is whether you received it at or about the time it was prepared, in June 1995?
>
> A: I don't recall whether that just went to the Academic Affairs Committee or the full Board.
>
> Q: Do you remember seeing it yourself?
>
> A: I don't recall.
>
> Q: You don't remember?
>
> A: No. (Testimony, pp. 5546-47).

Abandoning Obligations

The growing strains between Adelphi's faculty and administration can be seen in the figures in table 6.4. This table shows the degree of agreement/disagreement by, on the one hand, faculty and, on the other hand, the administration/Board of Trustees on the most important personnel decisions—faculty promotions and the granting of tenure (or a permanent appointment) — in the mid-1990s, when the struggle between the two sides had become most pronounced and had begun to draw public attention.

It is not unusual for faculty and administration to be at odds over personnel matters; the extent, however, to which both sides were set against each other at Adelphi is extreme. At the majority of American institutions of higher learning, more often than not, faculty opinion prevails in cases of promotion and tenure; the more prestigious the institution, the more likely this is so. When academic administrators routinely overturn faculty recommendations, it is generally not a reflection of the quality of candidates, but almost always of a contentious climate on campus. Contrary to what is often said or written, academic administrators are not typically put in a position of having to uphold professional standards, although there is no denying that faculty personnel committees too often can be lax and erratic in their decisions and recommendations.

Table 6.4 makes clear once again that the administration and faculty at Adelphi could not work together, that shared governance had completely broken down—and that some of the most essential work of academic governance, retaining capable faculty—was not being done.

Indeed, table 6.4 would suggest that some among these highly educated and presumably rational adults—both senior faculty and administrators—preferred strife to compromise. Both sides often talked about precedent and principles as justification for what in numerous instances was simply capriciousness. The activist faculty were no less zealous than the administration. As one put it: "Sometimes, when you destroy a parasite when it's gotten this far into the body, you might lose the patient, but if you do nothing, you will *certainly* lose the patient."[9] Surely, more than a few untenured assistant professors soon to be on the job market might have had a different view of all the posturing and high-minded rationalizations.

The faculty and the administration both had a duty to objectively evaluate those being considered for promotion and tenure. Clearly, one or the other, or both, failed to do so. Once more, instead of adjudicating (or knocking heads together), as it should have, the Board of Trustees, almost consistently, blindly followed the lead of the Diamandopoulos administration.

Although most Trustees would not have the slightest idea of how to judge the quality of academic work (in the case of Adelphi, primarily one's teaching effectiveness, always a problematic matter to evaluate) —and it is perhaps best that they did not pretend to do so—it was pretty evident that the climate on campus was unhealthy. The Board of Trustees fell short in not protecting the right of junior faculty to a fair and professional assessment. Even during the hearings, the Board of Regents failed to grasp the vital and elementary fact that in this provincial battle of titans (or perhaps more accurately, Lilliputians) over power, little consideration had been given to these most vulnerable of faculty members. It was shameful, and inexplicable, how such a basic issue could be overlooked, particularly by senior faculty and experienced academic administrators who were practiced at pointing fingers, but unable to compromise. It is an excellent reflection of the level of bitterness that had permeated the Adelphi campus.

TABLE 6.4
Recommendations for Promotion (1992-1994)
and Tenure (1992-1995) at Adelphi

	Peer Review	Dean	Faculty Committee*	Provost	President	Board
Promotion						
Yes	14	6	10	3	3	3
No	0	8	3	11	11	11
Other			1 TIE			
Tenure						
Yes	29	19	25	12	12	12
No	1	7	4	18	14	13
Other		4 N/A	1	NO ACTION	4 N/A	5 N/A

* Faculty Committee on Retention, Tenure, and Promotion.

In these evaluations and decisions with regard to promotion and tenure, faculty were more often than not reversed by the central administration which was invariably supported by the Board. The deans' recommendations were often also ignored, which is always a sure sign to those familiar with academic life that something had surely gone wrong. There is little question that when faculty recommend fourteen individuals for promotion, but the provost, President, and the Board recommend only three, and that when faculty believe twenty-nine colleagues merit a continuing appointment, but the provost, President, and the Board concur in only 40 percent of the cases, collegiality on a campus is pretty badly frayed. There were countless explanations for this insidious infighting and impasse, all self-righteous and cloying.

The overwhelming rejection of the judgment of faculty shows that the fanciful talk about shared governance is frequently an empty platitude. A board's decision is final, and individual faculty harmed by the breakdown in professional behavior, civility, and common sense have little recourse.

In these episodes in the skirmish over power at Adelphi, a number of faculty members still early in their careers were the real losers. (Although it would be going much too far to draw an analogy between those who lost their jobs or whose careers were in other ways impaired and the casualties of war, there are some parallels here that give one pause.) There is no evidence that the more militant faculty, in spite of their legitimate moral indignation and the good they claimed they were doing for others, recognized this. The majority of Trustees, most of whom were socially privileged, unsurprisingly were completely oblivious to it. Most faculty and administrators involved in the impasse have no excuse.

Time best spent on teaching and scholarship was being wasted through internecine warfare. Academic life at Adelphi had reached its nadir. Given the distribution of power in American institutions of higher learning, there was little that could be done to convince both sides to cease and desist. The administration, with the backing of the Board, had no reason to; it could do pretty much as it wished. A surprising number of faculty seemed determined to ignore or were oblivious to this reality. They continued their campaign. Each action by one side generated a reaction from the other. Both were adept at passing resolutions, campaigning through the media, going to the courts for relief or for a dismissal, denouncing, vilifying, and unkindness. They were fairly evenly matched; the administration had control of the resources to punish faculty, while faculty were resolved to tie the administration in knots.

The struggle monopolized the time of many; it was a wonderful diversion for the campus politicians, those making a stand for faculty rights, or those defending administrative prerogatives. The more bitter the conflict, the more meaningful the life of campus intriguers, readily recruited to any cause, worthy or unworthy. They convinced themselves and others that what they were involved in was a virtuous crusade. For too many pursuing the academic calling, plotting and exchanging memoranda can be exhilarating. These activities are certainly less demanding than the tedium of engaging students' minds or scholarship. They are an all too common diversion in academia.

Sharing Power

Diamandopoulos was convinced that under weak executives and Trustees, administrative authority at Adelphi had eroded many years before his arrival, and from the beginning he had been determined to reclaim it. He believed that the faculty had slowly and systematically seized more power than was rightfully theirs. They did not seem to understand that policymaking was something delegated to the administration, not to them, but he would teach them this truth. Since so many faculty had tenure, it was difficult to control their excesses. In his mind, their union held them, the administration, and the University hostage. As he saw it, power was not shared as it should be; there was a lack of give-and-take: "There was no consultation. Collegial governance did not exist. Each faculty member defined his or her own educational mission. University-wide requirements for students were abolished." On their own, usurping the role of Trustees, the faculty were even "determining tenure and promotions."[10]

As faculty defiance escalated with each academic year, Diamandopoulos was more haunted by the idea that their power was excessive and had to be curbed. This obsession had perhaps become the guiding theme of his administration, at times overshadowing his will to remake Adelphi's academic program. On June 20, 1990, he proudly reported to the Board of Trustees: "A strong management team now runs the University.... The faculty has been controlled and directed; they are not running the University." Well into his administration dominating the faculty still possessed him. At a Board meeting on September 27, 1995, he told the Trustees:

> The curricular issue is the one that involves the faculty. There are different views on how one treats faculty. I have very strong views. The approach we initiated ten years ago did pay off, we stabilized the University; we restored the power of the Board; we now have a philosophy. We are going to address the question of the faculty. At the end of this academic year, we will be coming to the end of the faculty contract. There is only one body that runs this University, the Board. The President acts on behalf of the Board.

Although this was far from the reality at Adelphi, many Trustees must surely have welcomed these words.

When the Washington office of the American Association of University Professors informed the University that it was breaking off its investigation into Adelphi's personnel plan after some faculty had been denied tenure, Diamandopoulos responded: "The decision of the national AAUP not to publish a report on our practices is as irrelevant to the University's achievements as a decision to publish them would have been. We categorically reject the notion that uninvited outside organizations can arrogate to themselves the judgment of what is best for Adelphi, or that it matters to anyone whether or not you choose to maintain a 'watchful interest in developments at Adelphi.'"[11] Given the lengthy record of his poor judgment, nothing good could be expected, nor was it forthcoming.

In 1991, when the faculty and the University came to terms on new Articles of Governance and Provisions of Peer Review as part of a collective bargaining agreement, there was a feeling on the part of many at Adelphi that the worst was over. The powers of the faculty, the President, and the Board had been defined. Adelphi could now be governed collegially.

The truce, however, did not last long. Making demands about the Faculty Senate agenda that they knew the administration would find unacceptable, activist faculty had set a trap. As anticipated, always intemperate and foolish, Diamandopoulos took the bait. At the beginning of the fall semester of 1995, in a six-page letter to the University community, he formally severed relations with the Faculty Senate and described the policy wherein the faculty would be required to go through him to communicate with the Board of Trustees.

> But as I began to plan for the first faculty meeting of the year, I discovered that even before students and faculty have returned to campus the Senate executive committee is already insisting on an agenda that I sincerely believe to be inflammatory, absolutely contrary to the well-being of the University, and therefore an agenda that I cannot embrace.

> Neither, however, do I wish to engage in any more fruitless disputes about process or in the easy-to-come-by quarrels to which we have been prone—all deflecting us from our primary task....

> In the summer you received a resolution passed by the Board of Trustees rejecting certain communications sent to the Board by the Senate executive committee [SEC]. The SEC tried to subvert the office of the President by going immediately to the members of the Board in an attempt to have the Board direct University policy in accord with the interpretations and agenda of the SEC and contrary to the conception of the President....

> The Board, as the legal agent of the public trust in governing the University, believes that the authority of a President enjoying the trust and support of the Board encompasses the authority of a serious, committed, and caring faculty.

The faculty expresses itself to the Board through the President; the Board speaks to the faculty and acts through the President. ... The President entertains arguments and criticisms, weighs and consults—but finally he must act....

But if the Senate executive committee wishes to pursue a radically different agenda [than that of the administration] in formal forums, or to conduct discussions in my absence, I have decided that the best way to avoid rancorous procedural tiffs is, for the time being, not to exercise my right to approve agendas of the faculty meeting. If the SEC must have formal meetings on topics that I am convinced cannot but deflect us, I have concluded it is pointless for me to attempt to reason them into another way of thinking, or to place formal hurdles in the way of such vain gatherings. Let these meetings take place without me or "my administration"—but as formal meetings of the faculty, nonetheless. I will weigh the recommendations of such gatherings when they are formally submitted to me for action in accordance with University governance requirements.[12]

Few seemed upset that hostilities had again escalated. Faculty could sustain the claim that they were holding the high ground, struggling against tyranny. President Diamandopoulos could sustain the image that he was a firm and decisive manager. He could also polish the image that he was not a mere politician, but a statesman who would stay above pointless acrimony.

Diamandopoulos's imperiousness and willfulness here are hardly surprising. It is incomprehensible that faculty could actually have believed that going over the head of the President to the Board, given the comfortable relationship between the two, to resolve governance issues would have any outcome other than absolute repudiation. At the same time, the faculty obviously knew their man—Diamandopoulos would surely do something rash—and perhaps are deserving of some praise for this. To suggest that they could have been convinced there was some chance of succeeding here, is to suggest that they were all abysmally foolish, a conclusion that is not very likely, but not completely untenable.

Crisis in Management, and Beyond

In light of the sore disappointments for faculty political dabblers in their many skirmishes with the President, an increasing number of their peers who generally ignored campus squabbles were being drawn into the quagmire. An increasing number also grew truculent. They called twice for Diamandopoulos's resignation.

At the March 7, 1989 faculty meeting, there was an agenda item "crisis in management," which was to be a critical examination of

Diamandopoulos's overall performance as President. Before particulars of a report prepared by an ad hoc committee could be discussed and debated, Diamandopoulos and other administrative officers took their leave. The committee chair proceeded to summarize what seventy witnesses had told him and his colleagues. Among the points he made were: many—faculty, students, and former administrators—felt insulted and threatened by Diamandopoulos's inner circle; some reported that their programs were being destroyed; most agreed that Diamandopoulos was intolerant, and surrounded himself with sycophants; former administrators found him uncollegial; and, contrary to University policy, the administration, without formal or informal consultation, was, on its own, hiring new faculty.

A motion was then made that "the faculty request and urge that the Board of Trustees remove and replace the President and acting provost as expeditiously as possible." On a voice vote, 93 supported the motion, and 43 opposed it; by secret ballot, 110 were in support, while 40 opposed it.

In a second vote of censure in October 1995, there were three separate motions. The first called for "the immediate resignation of the President, Peter Diamandopoulos." It was passed by a lopsided 131 to 14 margin, with 6 abstentions. The second recommended "the public disclosure by the Board of Trustees of all records related to fiscal decisions during the President's tenure." This was supported by 140 faculty. A companion resolution proposed that a joint committee of Trustees, faculty, students, alumni, and community leaders investigate the charges of mismanagement of the University. It passed 140 to 7, with 4 abstentions. The Board of Trustees, as it did after the first vote in 1989, saw this as yet another burden imposed on President Diamandopoulos's personal life and accordingly increased his compensation.

Actually, there was a third referendum. On February 6, 1996, the executive committee of the Faculty Senate passed a resolution demanding the immediate resignation of the officers of the Board of Trustees, and individual members Hilton Kramer, George Lois, and John Silber, as well as senior vice president Igor Webb and treasurer Catherine Hennessy.

Diamandopoulos responded to the growing criticism with more defiance and irascibility. He continued to refuse to meet with representatives of the Faculty Senate, as well as with almost all faculty delegations. He refused to take seriously the reservations and concerns of anyone not totally committed to his short- and long-term plans. He rejected a number of faculty overtures to talk and work together. He did not believe that they had been made in good faith and were serious. He was probably correct. He took the unusual step of completely eliminating the Faculty Senate's budget. He and his defenders continued to declare academic successes even when there was no evidence of them. There is absolutely no way of ascertaining whether or not they truly believed all of their claims. Their certainty that faculty were out to sabotage, for the right or wrong reasons, all of their efforts was surely true. (This was used as a rationale for their many failures, almost all of which would have occurred with or without faculty help.)

The Faculty's Fate

Declining enrollments and the resulting budgetary concerns necessitated the loss of full-time faculty. Table 6.5 shows that Adelphi's faculty shrank by sixty-two positions between 1983 and 1992. This is a reduction of 19 percent in nine years. The marked decrease in the rank of associate professor can in part be explained by the figures in table 6.4, which show how few faculty members (assistant and associate professors) were promoted or given tenure during these years, and in part by individuals at this rank still having employment opportunities at other institutions.[13]

TABLE 6.5
Number of Full-Time Faculty, Adelphi University,
1983-1984 and 1992-1993*

Rank	Number, 1983-1984	Number, 1992-1993	% Change
Professor	107	100	-6.5
Associate Professor	118	87	-24.3
Assistant Professor	92	80	-13.0
Instructor	12	0	
Total	**329**	**267**	**-19.0**

* These particular years were used as these were the most complete and reliable data that could be found.

Sources: *Academe*, Volume 70, Number 2, July/August 1984, p. 43; and *Academe*, Volume 79, Number 2, March/April 1993, p. 59.

It is hardly surprising that a faculty seeing a decrease in its size of this magnitude would feel threatened and, if nothing else, would raise its voice. The reaction of the faculty at Adelphi was about what one would expect from employees facing retrenchment. When will the cuts abate? How deep will they go? What departments will be hit the hardest? Most importantly: Who's next? (Actually, after 1992, the number of faculty continued to decrease.)

Some faculty members may have an abiding interest in abstruse educational philosophies and principles. Some faculty members may have an unrestrained lust for power. Some faculty may get caught up in the fervor of campus politics. Almost all faculty, however, are concerned with holding on to their jobs—to advance their professional lives, to help feed their families. An academic administrator who does not understand this simple truth is at least guilty of being completely out of touch with academic culture, even humankind. Great arrogance, simple-mindedness, or single-mindedness might explain, but would not excuse, this lapse. Nonetheless, not to know this should, if nothing else, disqualify someone from holding a position of leadership, whether in an institution of higher learning or elsewhere.

Between 1985 and 1995, the percentage of the budget devoted to instructional expenses at Adelphi decreased by nearly 15 percent. Class sizes were increased. Underused dormitories were closed, as was the school's radio station. The number of courses offered was reduced. While the administration grew by between 250 and 300 percent, student services were cut. Many of the professional programs were eliminated. Support staff were laid off. Library acquisitions were curtailed, and at times halted. Departmental budgets were cut; copier paper became so scarce it had to be rationed. Diamandopoulos related his accomplishments to the Board. It encouraged Diamandopoulos to press ahead with his program to remake Adelphi.

The 1987 Adelphi tuition of $7,272 nearly doubled by 1995. Over eleven years, tuition skyrocketed approximately 140 percent; in a five-year period in the early 1990s, it was raised 60 percent, making it more expensive than its local competitors, C. W. Post College and Hofstra University. It was becoming obvious that the State University of New York at Stony Brook—less than thirty-five miles away from Garden City, with an administration less unhinged, a more renowned faculty, and tuition a fraction of Adelphi's—would be a better choice for any student who qualified for admission. Just as significant, parents, regardless of economic means, also were becoming aware of this.

Rather than attaining the goal of turning Adelphi into an elite liberal arts college, the Diamandopoulos administration could not afford to become more selective in its admission standards. In spite of liberal scholarships to recruit (some said to purchase) students with relatively high SAT scores for the Honors College, the average scores of freshmen increased only slightly from 903 in 1988 to 942 in 1995. Of the 1,947 individuals who applied to Adelphi in 1996-1997, 1,387 or 71 percent were accepted. Fewer high school students were choosing to enroll at Adelphi once they were admitted. In 1987, 42 percent of those accepted enrolled; by 1991, the figure had dropped to 37 percent. It continued to fall: in 1992, it was 29 percent; in 1993, it was 27 percent; in 1994, it was 26 percent; in 1995, it was 24 percent. The high school rank of those admitted in that year was 27 percent in the top tenth, 55 percent in the top quarter, and 83 percent in the top half.

Only Adelphi's tuition soared, not its academic reputation.[14] Diamandopoulos and his diminishing number of acolytes blamed it all on faculty resistance. Most importantly, the Board continued to believe in, and to defend, him. His reports to them were always soaring and self-laudatory. His aspirations seemed boundless. Since most Trustees knew little about academic life and had little inclination to learn even the most rudimentary facts about the reality at Adelphi, what he said was not challenged.

The Trustees could not understand how faculty, whose salaries had increased so much during Diamandopoulos's tenure, could be so ungrateful and recalcitrant. He had worked to make their lives more comfortable. (Of course, over the years the gap between his salary increases and the faculty's grew, but this was initially not known even to most of the Trustees.) Yet, the Board was now convinced that an ineffectual faculty always put its petty self-interests and grievances before the needs of Adelphi.

As can be seen in table 6.6, faculty salaries at Adelphi had increased a great deal in the late 1980s and early 1990s, but they also increased across the country, and the Adelphi faculty had not become relatively better off than their counterparts on other campuses.

TABLE 6.6
Average Faculty Salaries, Adelphi University, 1983-1984 and 1992-1993

Rank	Salary, 1983-1984	Rating*	Salary, 1992-1993	Rating*
Professor	$39,200	3	$62,400**	3
Associate Professor	$30,200	3	$49,200**	2
Assistant Professor	$25,400	2	$40,700**	3

* This rating of average salary represents the percentile interval: The number 2 is between the 80th and 60th percentiles; the number 3 is between the 60th and 40th percentiles.

** The purchasing power in 1983-1984 dollars of a professor's salary of $62,400 would have been $44,868, an increase of 14 percent over $39,200; of an associate professor's salary of $49,200 would have been $35,376, an increase of 17 percent over $30,200; of an assistant professor's salary of $40,700 would have been $29,265, an increase of 15 percent over $25,400.

Sources: *Academe*, Volume 70, Number 2, July/August 1984, p. 42; and *Academe*, Volume 79, Number 2, March/April 1993, p. 58.

Between 1983 and 1992, the average salary of professors at Adelphi grew by $23,200 or 59 percent, the average salary for associate professors by $19,000, or 63 percent, and the average salary for assistant professors by $15,300, or 60 percent. As large as these figures may appear, when viewed against average faculty salaries nationwide, they were in no way exceptional. The percent increase in faculty salaries nationally for that period was as follows: 1983: 4.7 percent; 1984: 6.6 percent; 1985: 6.1 percent; 1986: 5.9 percent; 1987: 4.9 percent; 1988: 5.8 percent; 1989: 6.1 percent; 1990: 5.4 percent; 1991: 3.5 percent; 1992: 2.5 percent. This total of 51.5 percent (not compounded) is not as sizable as the average salary increases of 60 percent at Adelphi, but casts the latter in a new light; they certainly appear not to be as liberal as some may have believed.

Adelphi faculty had no particular reason to believe that the salary increases they were receiving were in any way magnanimous. From table 6.6 it can be seen that, relative to associate professors at other institutions, associate professors at Adelphi had made some gains in the ten-year period. At the same time, comparatively, (full) professors had not moved up or down, while assistant professors had actually lost ground.

Finally, according to the Bureau of Labor Statistics, during this period the Consumer Price Index increased by slightly more than 38 percent (not compounded)—1983: 3.8 percent; 1984: 3.9 percent; 1985:

3.8 percent ; 1986: 1.1 percent ; 1987: 4.4 percent; 1988: 4.4 percent; 1989: 4.6 percent; 1990: 6.1 percent; 1991: 3.1 percent; 1992: 2.9 percent. The rate of inflation essentially wiped out a substantial portion of the salary raises received by the Adelphi faculty; the "real" salary increase was closer to 15 percent rather than 60 percent, which is neither insignificant nor remarkable. In spite of what some Trustees said in their testimony before the Board of Regents and in other forums and what the administration told the media, economically the Adelphi faculty had no reason to feel beholden to President Diamandopoulos or to the Board. It was now obvious that President Diamandopoulos was able to balance the budget only by continuing to reduce the percent of expenditures allocated to instruction. The prospect for faculty was a smaller piece of the pie, which was clearly getting smaller.

Adelphi's Reputation

On the face of it, the very public feuding between the administration and the faculty at Adelphi over the curriculum, and control of the school in general, seemed certain to damage the institution's reputation. And in some circles it did, as seen in declining student enrollments, its inability to attract and hold students—good or mediocre. Incompetent administration and self-destructive bickering had taken their toll, and rationalizations that reducing the size of the student body was by design rang hollow. Adelphi had become less competitive. Publications which provide information about institutions for high school guidance counselors and students and their parents seeking facts and figures about different undergraduate programs—regardless of their true value—reflected precisely this.

Table 6.7 shows how Adelphi's competitiveness was rated by perhaps the most highly regarded and widely read publications by high school counselors and the general public, *Barron's Profiles of American Colleges.*

Adelphi's diminished ranking in competitiveness, from being very competitive to being less competitive during Diamandopoulos's presidency shown in table 6.7 is more evidence that his effort to turn Adelphi into an elite liberal arts college which would attract bright and motivated students was a failure. Indeed, to avoid insolvency, it became necessary to lower admission standards. The scholarships

TABLE 6.7
Barron's Assessment of Adelphi's Competitiveness, 1986-1996

Year/Edition	Rating*
1986/Fifteenth	Very Competitive
1988/Sixteenth	Very Competitive
1990/Seventeenth	Very Competitive
1991/Eighteenth	Very Competitive
1992/Nineteenth	Competitive + (Plus)
1994/Twentieth	Less Competitive**
1996/ Twenty-First	Less Competitive

* In this guide, colleges are rated from highly competitive (those that "look for students with grade averages of B+ to B and accept most of their students from the top 20 percent to 35 percent of the high school class") to noncompetitive (those which "generally only require evidence of graduation from an accredited high school").

** "These colleges usually admit 85 percent of their applicants."

awarded to attract the handful of superior students (by Adelphi standards) to the Honors College depleted the school's thin financial reserves even more quickly. The faculty continued to grumble and make mischief at every opportunity, the President became more authoritarian and promised success with time to spare, and the Board of Trustees passed resolutions commending the President's and its own putative accomplishments.

At the same time, the determination of the Diamandopoulos administration to require all undergraduates to take some of their course work in the traditional liberal arts, the demeaning of those who espoused a curriculum giving more attention to America's diverse ethnic, religious, and cultural heritage, the unrelenting verbal barrage against the professoriate, and the courting of reactionary and conservative public figures caught the attention and earned the praise of the political Right.

Adelphi was one of only fifty-eight institutions (along with, alphabetically, Asbury, Assumption, Baylor, and Birmingham-Southern) recommended in the second edition of *The National Review College Guide: America's Top Liberal Arts Colleges.*[15] The editors point out that President Diamandopoulos "has transformed this once-sleepy commuter college into one of the East's most dynamic universities."

> He's a hero, right? To us, yes, but not necessarily to the educational establishment, or even to his own faculty. The thing about Dimo, as the President is known around campus, is that he says what he thinks, and he does what he

says, and the faculty at Adelphi was used to administrators they could push around.... And sure enough, in 1989 the faculty voted no confidence in Diamandopoulos, and observers of higher education were confidently predicting his early retirement. The President replied that such votes are "the commonest, most ordinary, and most pedestrian routine that faculty resort to in weak institutions throughout America."...

Those that suppose that colleges cannot change for the better have only to turn to Adelphi for an example to the contrary. Under the Diamandopoulos presidency, just about everything about the School has been upgraded: the quality of the incoming students; the quality of the faculty (in part through stricter rules for granting tenure); and the quality of its curriculum.... [P]lease note that the School's expansion has been accompanied by the elimination of its debts and the tripling of its endowment. Bucking the national trends, enrollment is up; SAT scores are up; every newly hired professor (more than seventy of them) has a Ph.D.... If that's not enough to get the juices flowing, imagine this: more than seventy administrators were either fired or resigned, and many will not be replaced.[16]

The editors conclude their homage promising to "be keen observers of Adelphi's continued, astonishing growth."[17]

This misrepresentation of the reality of Adelphi apparently did little to change Diamandopoulos's or the school's waning fortunes in attracting students. The direction of enrollments did not change until after Diamandopoulos was removed as President. Perhaps some awestruck high school seniors concluded, after reading this panegyric, that it would be a waste of time to apply to such a distinguished institution; they would never be admitted. Whatever the case, one of the editors did benefit from this work. He was hired by President Diamandopoulos to teach creative writing, a subject in which he obviously had considerable skill.

The University was also able to attract some funds from organizations which embraced conservative causes. The National Endowment for the Humanities, while headed by the Republican Party activist Lynne V. Cheney, directed a government grant to Adelphi to support President Diamandopoulos's initiatives. The John M. Olin Foundation, of which William E. Simon was president, and which is widely known as a sponsor of right-leaning institutions, for example, the National Association of Scholars, the Hudson Institute, and Hilton Kramer's *New Criterion,* and individuals, for example, Charles Murray, Ronald Radosh, and Allan Bloom, gave the University a grant to hire faculty to teach in the newly developed programs.

Public figures from the far right of the political spectrum, like Judge Robert Bork, were brought to campus to lecture. Honorary degrees were awarded to others with similar political views, such as William F. Buckley, Jr., Richard Cheney (Lynne V. Cheney's husband), Paul Johnson, Max Kampelman, Peggy Noonan, and Richard Pipes. President Diamandopoulos also recruited high-profile faculty and administrators with right-leaning ideology and connections, for example, Carnes Lord, who had been a national security advisor to Vice President Quayle, Bruce Bawer, who had been an editor of the *New Criterion,* Mark Blitz, who had been a public policy analyst at the Hudson Institute, and Ronald Radosh. These steps did not result in an increase of Adelphi's endowment, but they did contribute to the growing estrangement between the school's faculty and administration. Adelphi was becoming identified as a creation of individuals whose educational agenda was secondary to their political agenda.

Looking at the entire record, Diamandopoulos's achievements at Adelphi were few. He and the Trustees dissipated a good deal of power and resources overreaching and in pursuit of a chimera. There were too many obstacles to impede their grand design; not least of all was the embittered and recalcitrant faculty.

Still, there were many who were convinced that the critics were simply on a witch-hunt. As they saw it, the imbalance of power at Adelphi was less of a concern than the unbalanced attacks on the Board and Diamandopoulos. They were strong defenders of the Diamandopoulos years. Their counterattack was not always truth-filled, but always impassioned.

Notes

1. Christopher Elias, "Lesson on Governance for a College," *Insight* Volume 7, Number 15, 15 April, 1991, p. 60.
2. Marilyn Goldstein, "2 Problem Schools, 2 Problem-Solvers: Diamandopoulos of Adelphi," *Newsday,* 6 June, 1986.
3. Minutes of the Meeting of the Adelphi University Board of Trustees, 1 December, 1993, pp. 2-3.
4. Emily Eakin, "The Right School?: The Oracle at Adelphi," *New York Magazine,* 16 October, 1995, p. 43. There was an awareness on the part of the Adelphi Board of Trustees and administration of the school's "less than exemplary tradition of fundraising." For the fiscal year 1993-94, the school "established a financial goal of $2.2 million" which it characterized as "extremely ambitious," but by almost any standard would be considered quite modest. (Minutes of the Meeting of the Adelphi University Board of Trustees, 1 December, 1993, p.6). As it turned out, that year Adelphi raised only about two-thirds of this amount.
5. Exhibit, P-332.
6. Exhibit, P-333.

148   **When Power Corrupts**

7. Exhibit, P-334.
8. Exhibit, P-335.
9. Quoted in Courtney Leatherman, "A President under Fire: Professors at Adelphi U. Try to Oust Diamandopoulos from Office," *Chronicle of Higher Education,* 3 November, 1995, p. A24.
10. Elias, "Lesson on Governance for a College," op. cit.
11. Letter from Peter Diamandopoulos to B. Robert Kreiser, 7 January, 1991. Diamandopoulos took pride in what he saw as his toughness, and was not reluctant to repeat publicly this type of gratuitous rudeness. See Elias. "Lesson on Governance for a College," p. 61.
12. Peter Diamandopoulos, An Open Letter from the President, 25 August, 1995. Diamandopoulos's unusual communication was buttressed by a move taken by the Board of Trustees two months earlier. On June 28, 1995, The Board of Trustees responded to a letter and documents supporting objections to launching the Honors College sent to it by the Faculty Senate by unanimously passing a resolution which stated, in part: "1. The only channel of communication between the Board of Trustees and the faculty of Adelphi University is through the office and person of its President." It is inconceivable that the faculty would not anticipate that the Board would see this ploy in the continuing war of nerves as yet another lese majesty—against both it and the President—and would be less than accommodating.
13. For a variety of reasons—most particularly their high academic salaries—full professors without great professional visibility are rarely recruited to other institutions. They are less mobile than assistant or associate professors. Moreover, since essentially all full professors have tenure, few are ever terminated.
14. Tuition was also skyrocketing at most other private institutions across the country.
15. Charles J. Sykes and Brad Miner, Editors, *The National Review College Guide: America's Top Liberal Arts Schools,* New York: Simon & Schuster, 1993.
16. Ibid., pp. 31-32.
17. Ibid., p. 34.

7

The Counterattack:
Defending the Board and President

Another View

For those encouraged by the changes that had been made at Adelphi between 1985 and 1995, there was no reason to investigate the Board of Trustees with regard to misconduct, neglect of duty, or failure to pursue or carry into effect the educational mission of the University. The Board, with the authority and responsibility to set Adelphi's course, had been remarkably successful in doing so. It could be faulted for nothing more than thwarting the will of a handful of perennially discontented faculty who mistakenly believed that this was their responsibility. As far as the Board was concerned, when it and faculty committees disagree about priorities, it should prevail. Put most directly, the legitimacy of a board's actions in no way depends on the wishes or consent or satisfaction of faculty. In the hierarchy of authority, the governing board is at the apex. When a board takes a position, faculty must accede. Duly elected governing boards, not faculty committees, run institutions of higher learning.

The Adelphi Board acknowledged that the faculty could and should contribute to furthering the University's goals. This, however, could not be taken to mean that the latter could unilaterally determine or define these goals and the University's mission. As the name implies, this is what governing boards do. They directly and indirectly govern by appointing and overseeing those who manage; they also plan the future of a college or university. It seemed obvious enough: how could anyone not see how American institutions of higher learning work?

The Board of Trustees and other allies of Diamandopoulos had an overwhelming desire to believe in his wizardry. Over the years, he had created a cultlike following. Those swept up by his predictions of greatness attributed untold powers to him. His causes became their causes, his hurts a source of their pain. They seemed horrified by the idea that anyone could find fault with him. Those not taken up by his enthusiasms were apparently not thinking or seeing clearly. In any event, it was not the place of faculty to question him; they should be willing to make contributions to and sacrifices for him and his programs, and for Adelphi. Diamandopoulos's friends were true friends, committed to defending him against his enemies, those who went public with their doubts.

Some faculty at Adelphi were less in a rush to believe, were not intoxicated by the elixir and were determined to take their governing role well beyond what the Board had ceded, and, not surprisingly, everything that they said and did was seen as a menace. To many Trustees, they were not merely skeptics, but dangerous agitators. They were not only making a career disagreeing with Board-approved programs and initiatives, but were going to great lengths to undermine them. They had created a great deal of dissension on campus, and over time this had escalated to constant, disturbing, and all too visible unrest. Their number had become too large to ignore. Now the demons were attempting to demonize. Fair-minded outsiders needed to know this. Never wincing, Diamandopoulos held his ground, counterpunched, and kept the loyalists together:

> Ironically, perhaps, "the strife and antagonism" to which you allude are the direct consequence of the incessant and virulent attacks on the administration, the Trustees, and ultimately the University itself by the leadership of the Adelphi AAUP [union] chapter. Not only have false, malicious, and defamatory charges of unlawful conduct been fed to the media and others, but also the mere existence of these allegations is then used as the basis for demanding the resignation of the members of the administration and the Board of Trustees of this private University.[1]

As the Board saw it, in their efforts to move the University in a different direction, the faculty leadership was willfully defying the wishes of duly empowered authority, and cynically twisting and distorting the truth. The Trustees were truly shocked that they were being attacked, at how obdurate and nasty faculty had become, and at how determined faculty were to get their way regardless of the consequences. To them, the charges raised against the President, and the Board, were at bottom unfounded and without merit. That there was a crisis was a falsehood. Faculty were harming the reputation of a dedicated administration and a dedicated and generous Board whose sole interests were improving the fortunes and future of Adelphi. The results of the faculty misbehavior would be irreparable harm to the University.

There was never a hint that any of the Trustees, President Diamandopoulos's inner circle, and other allies saw matters differently. They were convinced that their cause was pure, and they would be just as passionate about it as the troublemakers were about theirs. Diamandopoulos played on this allegiance by insisting that the Faculty Senate and the union leadership were the real enemy. This gave the faithful something concrete to rally around, something to keep them united. In addition to this cadre of faculty, liberals and the media they manipulated became part of the us-versus-them dynamic.

The Committee to Save Adelphi

From the beginning through the end (and beyond), the Committee to Save Adelphi was dismissed by Diamandopoulos and the Board as little more than "a union front" set on blocking all of the Diamandopoulos administration's efforts to revamp the curriculum and upgrade academic standards. The Committee only coalesced after it became clear that the faculty union would not gain full control of all facets of the academic program. It was then that the Committee set upon its course of sabotage, of utilizing "negative publicity based on lies, distortions, and disinformation" to undercut the accomplishments of the Board and the Diamandopoulos administration. To the Trustees, the who, why, and what of the Committee were transparent: "For the past year and a half, Adelphi has been subjected to a well-financed 'corporate campaign' by a small group of dissidents, mainly the directorate of the faculty union, who have long been seeking to gain control of campus policy."

Initially, the Adelphi administration and Board indicated that they would welcome a Board of Regents' inquiry into the complaints of the Committee to Save Adelphi. The contention was that the accusations by the Committee were "based either on misinformation, misinference, misunderstanding, or outright lies." Senior vice president Igor Webb spoke for the administration and the Board: "At last the University can face and interrogate its accusers under oath, dismantle the charges one by one, and demonstrate their falsehood."[2]

The Trustees issued a statement predicting that a fair investigation "will vindicate management practices and Board leadership." As Webb put it,

> Reckless attempts by a group of dissident faculty at Adelphi to undermine those relationships [with influential and accomplished men and women who as Trustees assist not-for-profit institutions] as part of their campaign to unseat the President and the Board and, in effect, seize control of Adelphi must be recognized for what they are, and not allowed to succeed.

In their counteroffensive, the Diamandopoulos administration steadily increased its efforts to discredit its opponents. All criticism was dismissed as merely an immature attempt "to embarrass and humiliate the President publicly." According to the official University spokesman, vindictive faculty were "preying on a culture of envy;" what was being witnessed was nothing more than an attempt to derail sound educational changes; the President was being punished for his efforts "to stem the tide of political correctness and multiculturalism," as these were proving to be the ruin of serious education and scholarship in American colleges and universities. Moreover, "the faculty are pissed because they don't run the University."

In the eyes of the Trustees, the economic picture at Adelphi had never been brighter. The administration was in excellent hands. The clamor surrounding President Diamandopoulos's salary was artificial. In a statement issued by the chair and the Executive Committee of the Board on October 2, 1995, it vigorously made clear its view on this matter:

> The President's pay, in the view of the Board, precisely reflects his merits and his achievements as a unique educational leader. The story of the turnaround at Adelphi that he has led is extraordinary. We believe he deserves every penny of his salary.... Adelphi is today at the forefront of educational innovation.... All of this is due directly to the inspired and courageous leadership of Peter Diamandopoulos. The real story at Adelphi is the story of a University in the strongest financial and academic condition in its one-hundred-year history. The Board of Trustees is extremely proud of what the President has been able to achieve both academically and financially. We intend to compensate the President for his services at a level that will ensure his continuing leadership of the University for many years to come.

Later that month, the Board passed another resolution unequivocally backing Diamandopoulos.

On January 16, 1996, the full Board once more publicly made the case for Diamandopoulos:

> Since this [October 2, 1995] statement was issued, the facts contained therein have been largely ignored. Instead, baseless and wildly inaccurate claims, many personally defamatory, have continued to appear in the national media. These claims have been made by a small group of individuals who, in order to promote their own agenda, have distorted the impressive record of accomplishments of Adelphi.... Clearly some feel threatened by the demanding academic standards being instituted by the President and the Board.... The Board of Trustees unconditionally affirms its confidence in President Peter Diamandopoulos and the philosophy, policies, and practices that, with the full support of the Board, he has vigorously pursued. The educational goals that the President and the Board have established, and the command of the institution by the President, cannot and will not be compromised.

President Diamandopoulos had provided a belief system and had given the Board a new faith to follow. In doing so, he had created a large number of disciples. The themes of their defense— Diamandopoulos had worked miracles, the criticisms were a tissue of lies, the critics were but a small number of faculty, Adelphi was well on its way to becoming an elite institution, the resistance to rigorous standards was what was motivating faculty, the leftward leaning faculty and media were conspiring to undo Diamandopoulos's achievements, and the clamor was but a union ploy—would be heard again and again in the attempt to justify Diamandopoulos's misadventures.

Diamandopolous's allies were many and determined. Their advocacy was ardent and direct. Igor Webb's response to the commentary about the President's compensation went further than what the Trustees independently and collectively had said: "The Board of Trustees are the people who employ him; it thinks he's entitled to this compensation, and whether the faculty or anyone else likes it or not is irrelevant. But that hasn't stopped the Regents, the attorney general, or the media from behaving in the most irresponsible manner.... I think the Regents do not have the right to drag the affairs of a private institution into public view." On the matter of the Board providing the condominium in Manhattan, Webb observed: "if the president of Brown comes to New York, he lives in an apartment. It's not a scandal, though, because it's Brown—he deserves it. If Adelphi is to try to claim to have programs that genuinely can be nationally competitive, the *New York Times* says we ought to offer our students only 'a taste of education' [vocationalism rather than an emphasis on the liberal arts]."[3]

Some Trustees Speak Out

Although some might believe it hardly possible, Trustee John Silber's assessment of the efforts of the Committee to Save Adelphi and the Regents' involvement was even more sweeping and less measured than the official array of comments. He saw the Committee, and what to him were gratuitously vicious actions of its leaders, as threats not only to Adelphi, but to the integrity of American higher education in general. He warned the Regents to ignore the Committee; if they did not, the poison it disgorged would infect them.

John Silber:

A: Can't the Board of Regents see through the sham, the Orwellian language of a Committee to Save Adelphi that's doing its best to destroy it? The Orwellian nature of the campaign should be enough to fail the smell test. You ought to be able to sniff the mendacity in this crowd. (Testimony, p. 2010)

A: See, I think the Board of Regents is involved in what is a work project by a union and are being, the attempt is being made to manipulate you and to misguide you with all kinds of things. You are so inundated with paper, how in the hell could you possibly get on top of all the issues that you have to face in sixteen meetings or in less than six or eight months? This effort to manipulate you by this group of people, it seems to me is shameful. And if they succeed in this, as I said in my earlier testimony, if they succeed in this, you will have changed collective bargaining totally in this country. From now on any faculty member will say, "what the hell are we doing fooling around at the bargaining table? All we do is we work out a media campaign."... It's easy to do it. You come up with our set of lies, you come up with an informed source, unnamed, has said; you don't say who it was, you don't say when it was, you don't say where it was.... The complexities of issues you have to face [are] all predicated on a bunch of goddamn lies. This, it seems to me, is truly outrageous. (Testimony, pp. 2012-14)

A: I would not describe it as a pimple. I would describe it as a rather large boil in a very sensitive spot that needs to be lanced. And once that boil is lanced, there will be a very fine and effective operating University.... The opposition and the turmoil have been created by this kind of guerrilla warfare in the media. But it is not the faculty.... But if the Regents come in and dismiss, don't think the boil is not going to be there, there will be a rash of boils throughout higher education in New York State and around the country. Because the new

techniques for collective bargaining will have been established.... And sometimes the right alternative, when truly immoral and sometimes illegal behavior
occurs, is to stamp that out and not to simply accommodate it. You can't
always appease people and succeed. I think you can learn that from the 1930s.
You don't appease certain power-mad individuals simply by acceding to them.
There is some point at which the authority, the proper authority that has been
entrusted to the Board of Trustees of Adelphi, has to be recognized and has to
be exercised. (Testimony, pp. 2015-19)

Silber was not the only Trustee to assail dissident faculty. In 1995,
Hilton Kramer weighed in with a double-barreled blast not only against
them but against the *New York Times* for furthering the cause of "a
few disgruntled faculty members" by publishing a "wildly distorted
report" on its front page.[4] Nothing in the charges or the newspaper—
"a hatchet job designed to malign the character and integrity of
Adelphi's remarkable President"—was reliable; it was all an "uncon-
scionably misleading account."

As Kramer saw it, Diamandopoulos's philosophy of education, which
"stands for elite teaching standards in the classroom," occasioned the
"implacably hostile coverage" by the liberal media. It is
Diamandopoulos's implementation of "high intellectual standards" that
"has gotten him into trouble with the liberals and leftists—first on the
Adelphi faculty and now at the *Times*": "All the phony talk about
money [the President's salary] is nothing but a smokescreen for an
attack on these standards, which are deemed to be too conservative
and elitist for the tenured radicals at Adelphi who prefer to wallow in
politically correct palaver about race, class, and gender":

Only a few months ago, the tenured radicals at Adelphi made a similar attempt
to destroy the new Honors College by demanding its dismantling, but they
failed to do so—and in their rage over that failure, they are now attempting to
discredit Dr. Diamandopoulos on money matters.

It is shameful enough for academics to engage in low-level politics of this
kind, but what is one to say about the *New York Times* for the way it has joined
in this assault on high intellectual standards? This is indeed an example of the
paper's current ideological derangement.

It is difficult to say what is more bewildering: to hear the desperate
and ineffectual faculty characterized as being a potent force in shaping Adelphi's policy or to hear the *New York Times* accused of "consistently" supporting "liberal nostrums."

Honorary Trustee, William E. Simon, former secretary of the treasury and president of the exponent of conservative causes, Olin Foundation, was another voice convinced that it would be a great public
disservice if Adelphi were diverted from the course it had set upon: "I
consider Peter a Renaissance man. He's fighting the conventional wisdom of tenure. He's not tolerating the liberal garbage that spews around.
He's hired teachers willing to teach freedom. If he stays for the next
ten years, Adelphi will be one of the best institutions in the country."[5]

The remarks of Peter Goulandris, the vice chair of the Board of
Trustees, sounded less fervent, but his judgment of the Committee to
Save Adelphi's activities was just as negative, and his convictions just
as strong.

Peter Goulandris:

Q: And can you tell me, when you say that the Board of Trustees has been
subjected to ad hominem attacks as part of a campaign, to whom do you
attribute the campaign, sir?

A: I attribute the campaign to a fringe group who are sadly misguided. As you
know, we have a union contract up this year; I view this as a — virtually, a
negotiating tactic that has gone way beyond the bounds of any norm of decency....

Q: And did you attach any significance to the fact that the faculty as a group
had voted to call for President Diamandopoulos's resignation?

A: Yes, I did. I viewed the significance as that of a pressure tactic in a game
that was being played out, and I even consider that to be improper. I think in an
institution such as this, we should be collegial, we should work together. Our
only job here as Trustees or as administrators is to educate young people and to
look after the welfare of the institution and its faculty, and we don't want to be
confrontational in that regard; we want to work together with people.... We
want to improve, we want to make positive changes, and sometimes a union
organization can be afraid of change, per se. It may not be bad, but they are
afraid of it; so they resist. And that has caused us great pain because there's no
reason why we can't be partners in an effort toward evolution and change
rather than adversaries....

Q: Mr. Goulandris, was there any discussion on the Board of Trustees to
opening a line of communication with the faculty of the University after September 30, 1995?

A: Ma'am, I'll tell you one thing, again, we're sort of constrained in a way by
the union bargaining process, because, in fact, you may know that the Board of
Trustees passed a resolution saying that Dr. Diamandopoulos represented the

University in dealing with the faculty, and there's a good reason for this: Because, if you are dealing with people who deal with you adversarily as opposed to collegially, you have to speak with one voice, you can't speak with five voices. (Testimony, pp. 2685-90)

Not all of the Trustees at Adelphi expressed negative views of faculty. Even the most sympathetic Trustees, however, were condescending, and none seemed able to fathom what was making faculty unhappy and rebellious. It was incomprehensible to them why powerless professionals, most often ignored and sometimes treated shabbily, might resist, turn to unionization, and create dissension. The Adelphi Trustees are not the only board in America to have been perplexed by this fairly predictable reaction.

Some Faculty Speak Out

Adelphi administration and Trustees were not alone in having serious misgivings about the faculty's unrelenting assault and tactics. In an interview with a newspaper reporter, the chair of the program of study in biology fretted: "The infighting is hurting the place."

Social scientist Edith Kurzweil, whose scholarship and work as an editor had earned her a modest international reputation before she was recruited to Adelphi by President Diamandopoulos as a University Professor, added to the defense of the Board and President.[6] Kurzweil confessed that she found the Regents' involvement and actions "shocking."

Like many committed scholars, Kurzweil had a generally low opinion of faculty campus politicians. She noted that those who eventually formed the Committee to Save Adelphi had long fought against the innovations to which the President was committed: "they felt threatened by the administration's push to raise standards, and by the (remote?) possibility that departmental structures might be altered." They had been engaged in "undermining distinguished visitors by steering students away from them, ignoring or insulting them, and insisting that their appointments not be renewed." They even encouraged students to transfer to other schools.

Kurzweil and other academics who shared her views were convinced that, given the resistance in American higher education to enforcing standards, Adelphi would not be able to effectively defend itself against the Committee's assault. She was convinced the spread of political correctness across America in the 1980s and 1990s had persuaded

many, on and off campus, that any sincere attempt to provide undergraduates with a true liberal arts education was a useless exercise.

Given the present climate, Kurzweil was also convinced that the
Regents' hearings could not possibly be unbiased, that they could best
be characterized as "a witch-hunt." If nothing else, she perhaps correctly predicted, the far-reaching consequences would enable educational bureaucrats to expand their reach: what has been happening
"has allowed special-interest politics to be confused with larger political questions, has converted educational issues into legal ones, and
has substituted ideology for standards."

Pessimistically, Kurzweil concluded that because those supporting
the status quo will stop at nothing to achieve their ends, from the start
the Committee to Save Adelphi was bound to succeed.

The wry observations of Maurice Cowling—a long-time Fellow at
Cambridge University and Distinguished Visiting Olin Professor at
Adelphi—were an even stronger indictment of the Committee to Save
Adelphi and the Board of Regents.[7]

Cowling begins his comments by praising President Diamandopoulos,
who, with "the brilliance of an outstanding personality," has worked
tirelessly "to create a properly academic institution out of the debt-ridden
institution" he inherited. He sees the President as "a man of eloquence,
vision, and ability [who] has clear ideas about what a university should
be" and the Adelphi campus as "a scene of turmoil and dispute." In
Cowling's mind, because it requires faculty to teach outside their special-
ties, the Honors College has especially fed the resentment of narrowly
trained faculty, not at all interested in broadening themselves or students. The relatively high salaries of some of the Honors College's more
visible appointments also increased the general level of discontent.

For Cowling, the most insidious development was the considerable
influence of "faculty and union leaders who by and large were radicals of the 1960s or later, and whose inclination to resist was intensi-
fied by the feeling that Dr. Diamandopoulos was an academic elitist
who was unfriendly to everything they stood for." When their repeated attempts to remove the President proved unsuccessful, these
provocateurs "enlisted the help of *Newsday* and the *New York Times*
(which both ran vicious campaigns against him)." The "slow drip of
public hostility" naturally took a toll.

> At the same time as the union's contract was coming up for renegotiation with
> the University, it [the Committee to Save Adelphi] mounted a pre-emptive

strike by launching a new attack in terms of financial corruption and appealing to the Regents of New York State with the request that they remove the Trustees from office.[8]

Cowling raises the specter that the Trustees were being ousted because of "the presence among the Regents of Democrats appointed by Mario Cuomo when he was Governor of New York,[9] or a ruthless exercise of newspaper power made more ruthless by the fact that [Trustee] Mr. Kramer, who had spent 17 years as art critic of the *New York Times,* has spent the last four years running a highly distinguished one-man newspaper campaign against the irresponsible, indiscriminate, and foolish liberalism of that newspaper. What is clear is that political animus has been present throughout." The Board of Regents has been behaving "more like a kangaroo court than a law court." To Cowling intervention by the Regents represents a far-reaching union victory, a "triumph for the know-nothing radical orthodoxy."

Roger Kimball, the managing editor of Hilton Kramer's *New Criterion,* repeated these same themes in the widely circulated *National Review,*[10] that the left-leaning press had spread untruths and had "conferred the appearance of legitimacy" on what were baseless rumors (creating "a textbook demonstration of...a show-trial by media"); that President Diamandopoulos's record was one of great accomplishments ("a striking success story") and essentially no failures; that the allegations were "groundless,"—"to the best of my knowledge, not a single charge was proved;" that there were only a handful of faculty with a political agenda who were "disenchanted" and "disgruntled;" that the fight was not really over educational issues but was a labor ploy—"a labor dispute masquerading as a battle over educational principles."

> For 12 years, Mr. Diamandopoulos took a stand against prevailing ideological fashions, especially the intellectually hollow demands for radical multiculturalism and political correctness. He strove to transform Adelphi from a third-rate commuter college into a respectable liberal arts institution.[11]

Faculty were in revolt only because "intellectual standards" were being set that were "higher than they were prepared to meet."

The Attorney General Speaks Out

Whatever the validity of any of the points in the resolute defense of the Board and the President, in the eyes of the law some of their actions had been illegal. Two years after the attorney general of the State of New York was asked to investigate matters at Adelphi in 1995, he brought suit against the (by then former) President and Trustees for "mismanaging the assets of the University...in violation of their fiduciary duties."[12]

Among other things, the complaint charged President Diamandopulos with "arranging and accepting without contemporaneous review by any but a handful of Trustees a package of salary, benefits, and perquisites not commensurate with services performed and unmatched by any leader of any comparable institution." The other Trustees are cited for "improperly allowing the President to amass that unreasonable compensation package, abdicating their responsibility to make informed decisions...and thereby failing to safeguard Adelphi's assets." Finally, according to the attorney general, "the former President and former Trustees also breached their duties of care and loyalty to the University by approving, or acquiescing in, business transactions between Adelphi and companies in which certain Trustees had a financial interest without ascertaining the true extent of those interests or confirming the fairness of the transactions to the University, resulting in an unwarranted personal benefit to those interested Trustees." The attorney general's brief asked that all misdirected assets be returned to Adelphi.

The official reaction by the University to the "outrageous inaccuracies foisted on the press...by the attorney general's office" was predictable: after it moved in the court to dismiss "certain subpoenas," it issued a press release accusing the government of filing papers containing "serious errors of fact and interpretation of the voluminous documents and sworn statements." The refutation was bitter and defensive:

> Igor Webb, senior vice president of Adelphi, today said, "it is obvious to Adelphi that the charities bureau [of the attorney general's office] has deliberately chosen to ignore direct sworn and documentary evidence which contradicts many of its expressed 'concerns' and which directly undercuts any need for further inquiry into a variety of areas. The release to the media of the filing is also obviously an effort to recycle by-now old allegations which the charities bureau has used for the last seven months to justify the existence of its inquiries and concerns which the University has already provided volumes of information.
>
> "Adelphi's view," he said, "firmly supported by law, is that the Board makes the decisions concerning the use of the University's assets, and not the attorney general. Having discharged its obligations pursuant to the law, the Board will

resist any 'second guessing' or attempt by the attorney general to substitute his political preferences for the judgment of the Board.

"Ultimately," he added, "we are convinced that the true story of Adelphi's renaissance over the past decade will be communicated to the public."...

According to Adelphi spokesman Vince Passaro, "the statement that appeared in documents given to the media yesterday, to the effect that the charities bureau has attempted to bring quick resolution to this star-chamber inquiry, is preposterous. Whoever composed such a statement looks at the truth from a distant, unfamiliar shore."...

The University remains absolutely confident that any proceeding governed by impartial rules of discovery, evidence, and law will vindicate its leadership, management, and record of achievement. For that reason, the University is determined to pursue its case.[13]

All attempts by the former Trustees to dismiss the core of the case were denied by the State Supreme Court.

The eventual unfavorable outcome for President Diamandopoulos and his Board to settle this claim (the chair of the new Board of Trustees described it as "an excellent settlement") is in some ways less important than its issuance.[14] It suggests that in the view of public officials, presumably neutral with regard to the conflict at Adelphi, there was more to the case than simply insubordinate or subversive or incompetent faculty intent on disrupting the plans of a right-minded Board and effective President.

A Final Attack

The Adelphi authorities used one additional stratagem to elicit support and lessen the possibility of removal by the Board of Regents. As the hearings were drawing to a close, they sent voluminous documents to members of college and university governing boards at other campuses which they were truly convinced exculpated them. The intent of this effort was to warn others that, if the Board of Regents could interfere with the internal affairs of Adelphi, they might be next, that a dangerous precedent was being set. The cover letters, signed by all of the Trustees, read, in part: "The hearings now under way...raise issues of utmost importance not just to Adelphi but to every institution of higher education in New York State, and to every current and prospective trustee of every such institution, now and in the future."

The most apparent effect of this tactic was that it greatly increased the number of people commenting on Adelphi's troubles, yielding even more unneeded publicity.

Notes

1. Letter from Peter Diamandopoulos to B. Robert Kreiser, 7 February, 1996.
2. Webb often communicated the Board's and President's response to the allegations to the public. For example, in a long opinion piece in the *New York Daily News* on August 25, 1996, he described the case against them as "a manufactured scandal" engineered by "private investigators and a press agent" on behalf "of a group of generously paid faculty members with guaranteed lifetime employment."

> This campaign is merely a new wrinkle in a 30-year-long practice at Adelphi, a University that historically, as one of its deans recently put it, "likes to eat its Presidents."...

> It is no coincidence that the leaders of the so-called Committee to Save Adelphi are the main players in Adelphi's faculty union, and that the law firm representing them for the Regents is also the faculty union's law firm in the ongoing contract negotiations.

> After years of deficits, institutional drift, and management by a militant faculty clique, Adelphi has, under President Diamandopoulos enjoyed growth in its endowment and reserves....

> The President and Board also have overhauled Adelphi's educational program....

> These changes have upset the routines and rituals of a faculty 80 percent of whom are tenured and some of whom have devoted their professional lives neither to scholarship nor teaching but to University politics. To recapture control of Adelphi, this group has made numerous false and damaging accusations and sensationalized the salary of the University President, who is entering his 12th year at Adelphi and his 46th as an educator.

> Enrolling a largely local student population, Adelphi educates the American middle class. A great deal of resentment apparently has arisen because Adelphi's President and Board have established for these students a rich education that genuinely can prepare them for the demands of our society, that can stir their dreams and ambitions, and that can challenge their intellects and their pride.

At every opportunity, this defense and attack were repeated.

Even when frustrated and perhaps disinclined, Webb acted as the primary spokesman to articulate the position of the Board and administration to the faculty. In a December 5, 1995 memorandum to the chair of the Faculty Senate, he, in part, wrote:

> It is time to be direct, however, about the realities of the moment. It is difficult to engage in serious dialogue with those in the faculty leadership who have undertaken a systematic campaign to vilify the University's chief officers and the University itself, who have resorted to false and malicious assertions to achieve their ends including what seems clearly to be libel and slander, and who have smeared the good name of the University in the public media. It is difficult to engage in serious dialogue when former members of the University community are being harassed by leaders of the so-called "Committee to Save

Adelphi" seeking to implicate these individuals in—or intimidating these individuals to implicate others in—alleged thefts or misappropriation of funds or other asserted illegalities. It is difficult to engage in serious dialogue when Tom Heffernan [a professor of English] writes to the U.S. Treasury Department brazenly claiming that the President is a thief and the newsletter of the so-called "Committee to Save Adelphi" then publishes the news that the IRS [Internal Revenue Service] is "interested" in Adelphi. It is difficult to engage in serious dialogue when months are devoted to amassing every rumor and fantasy concerning the leadership of the University and shamelessly feeding this false information to the press and the attorney general, so that it can be announced that the press and the attorney general are "investigating" Adelphi (which explains why for some time meetings between the SEC [Senate Executive Committee] and the administration not only have come to naught, but have had to be distorted in your memos to the faculty—since for these many months members of the SEC and the "Committee to Save Adelphi" were secretly plotting to bring down the administration, the President, and the Board). It is difficult to engage in serious dialogue when accusations of every species of personal misconduct are recklessly and heedlessly leveled against the President and other officers of the University. In the midst of this ugly, vicious, and disloyal campaign, it is, let's say, distasteful to find the SEC, the "Committee to Save Adelphi," and the faculty union—if indeed they are separate—clothing themselves in the language of integrity, quality, and standards.

3. Impugning the *New York Times* is a recurring theme of those denying any culpability on the part of the President or Board. For example, an article that did not reflect favorably on the chair of the Board brought forth the following immediate and sharp response from the Adelphi administration:

> Today's article on Mrs. Procope represents a further example of the *Times'* consistently biased coverage of the Adelphi situation. The article's misleading ambiguous headline ("Chairwoman of Adelphi's Board Is Accused of Using Her Double Role to Advantage") falsely insinuates that Adelphi's distinguished and accomplished chairman has been accused of wrongdoing by some party in a position of authority, when in fact, as is manifest in the article itself, the only criticism of Mrs. Procope and her firm has come from the self-interested individuals who call themselves the Committee to Save Adelphi.

> Moreover, the article itself devotes an amount of space usually reserved for major news stories in order to report, uncritically and in highly selective detail, this so-called Committee's baseless and irresponsible charges, to the effect that Mrs. Procope's firm has in some way unduly benefited from its long-standing relationship with the University.

> The facts about the Adelphi-E.G. Bowman relationship were presented in detail by Mrs. Procope, by Adelphi's vice president for finance and treasurer, and by others in recent testimony before the panel of the New York State Board of Regents. These facts, which the *New York Times*, notwithstanding its famous slogan, saw fit not to print, make it unmistakably clear to any objective observer that the Adelphi-Bowman relationship has at all times been at arm's length, has from day one brought significant financial and coverage related benefits to Adelphi, and has at all times been properly maintained with the full knowledge and consent of the Adelphi Board of Trustees.

To suggest otherwise—and, more particularly, to allow the pages of the *New York Times* to be used for what amounts to free advertising by a group of dissidents waging a propaganda campaign against Adelphi's administration and Board of Trustees—is a profoundly regrettable lapse from the *Times'* historically high journalistic standards.

This particular article elicited an even more spirited and, surely for those at the *New York Times*, bewildering response from an unexpected quarter. In a curious editorial in the *New York Amsterdam News*, its former publisher and husband of the chair of the Board of Trustees, Ernesta Procope, condemns the *Times'* reporting as racist, threatening to undermine his and his wife's ability as black entrepreneurs to compete in the insurance business:

The battle to dismantle the Adelphi Board of Trustees and oust its President, Peter Diamandopoulos, has turned into a public debacle which raises questions about racism and greed on a grand scale.

Recent attacks, the latest one in the *New York Times* Tuesday, September 24, seem to have reached a gloves-off fracas pitting a band of faculty dissidents against the University's administration. The question is why.

The beleaguered President, a Greek-American who has been on the job nearly 12 years, and the chairperson of the University's Board of Trustees, who is black, Ernesta Procope, seem to be the paramount targets of a witch-hunt perpetrated by a band of faculty members....

Procope, in addition to being the chair of the Board of Trustees, is one of the school's insurance brokers. Here's where the rub turns racial again—with the specious rationale that Procope made a million dollar profit on her business ventures with the school, calling it a conflict of interest.

In the *New York Times* article Monday, written by Bruce Lambert, the inference that Procope's firm, E.G. Bowman, did not earn its commission on its extensive policies, which any institution of higher education must have to stay in business, is erroneous according to my wife and I, who have led the firm to its Wall Street address and prestige as a mainstream American firm....

She [Procope] said the *New York Times* article obscures the fact that "my firm received a letter of authority from George Osborn, vice president of the University, appointing Bowman as its broker for the property-casualty program."

Is this too much for individuals at the *Times* and Adelphi who are out to undo African-Americans who are successful in the business world? Is this too much for a Greek-American who has raised the University's endowment from $4 million in 1985 to $50 million today? In hearings conducted and held before the Board of Regents for the past year or more, the Committee to Save Adelphi, according to the *New York Times*, said the Board of Trustees conferred its insurance business to E.G. Bowman without the Board's approval. All parties deny this allegation, but notes from this particular Trustee meeting have failed to turn up for inclusion in the record and transcript of the hearing....

Procope, according to the *Times,* was part of the Diamandopoulos lack of oversight duties, which the Committee listed among its grievances.

The University lost no time responding to the *New York Times,* saying the coverage of the hearings, in relationship to Procope, are "egregiously biased...." The statement also charges the *Times* with omitting part of the testimony, especially that which compliments Procope and refutes charges of duality, complicity, and favoritism....

Procope said, "I am outraged at the inferences published by the *New York Times* and I consider it an attack on my firm, because I am a black woman chairman of a white university, heading a black business attempting to operate in mainstream America."
(John Procope, "The Bowman-Procope Story: Running Blacks out of Business, a Cottage Industry for the *New York Times*?," 28 September, 1996, pp. 12, 43).

4. Hilton Kramer, "A Phony Issue at Adelphi," *New York Post,* 3 October, 1995, p. 17.
5. Emily Eakin, "The Right School?: The Oracle at Adelphi," *New York Magazine,* 16 October, 1995, p. 43.
6. Edith Kurzweil, "Regents' Decision Is a Blow to Education," *Newsday,* 12 February, 1997, A41-42. Kurzweil had published an earlier essay in *Newsday* on November 17, 1996 ("Is Diamandopoulos Getting a Bum Rap?") which was even less a defense of Diamandopoulos's "determination to bring about change at Adelphi" than an assault on her colleagues' "unprofessional behavior"—and the media's credulity. She insists that to understand events at Adelphi attention should be shifted from the President to the faculty.
    Kurzweil contends that behind the attacks on the University's administration is the desire on the part of faculty to dismantle the core curriculum so that they would be able to teach more "material from their own disciplines" and protect their narrow interests. She reports that smoldering dissatisfaction came to a head after "rumors began to be floated that the core curriculum, and the Honors College, which the faculty had approved, posed threats not only to departmental structures but to individuals' jobs."

    If the originally small group of professors who formed the Committee to Save Adelphi had not been able to create a climate of fear and suspicion, there would be no news stories. This Committee differs from groups of faculty who fight administrations at other universities: It met in secret during the entire summer and hired a public relations person to feed information to the press. The Committee later called faculty and other meetings a few times a week to inform on the President's "misdemeanors," while others tried to "get the two sides together." In the process, tenured professors were led to believe that unless they fought the administration to the bitter end, some colleagues might lose their jobs. Those colleagues who questioned the Committee were dubbed quislings....

    In sum, I deplore that the press has helped perpetuate a climate of opinion that focuses on the President's salary, and has chosen to overlook the aims and achievements of an inordinately courageous educator. Reporters have been duped. I only hope that the Board of Regents will find out why and how the

President's salary became an issue at all, and will call an end to these proceedings regarding allegations that the Adelphi Trustees acted improperly.

7. Maurice Cowling, "Peterhouse on Long Island," *Spectator,* Volume 278, 22 March, 1997, pp. 24-25.
8. Ibid., p. 25.
9. In fact, Regents are selected by members of the legislature.
10. Roger Kimball, "The Third Degree," *National Review,* Volume 49, Number 4, 10 March, 1997, pp. 31-32.
11. Ibid., p. 32. Actually, this is Kimball's second jab at the press and the Adelphi faculty. In November 1995, he wrote that the "barrage [of criticism has been] misguided and often intemperate." Not only did he implicate the *New York Times,* but he referred to an article in *New York Magazine* [see note 5 above] as a "nasty piece of gossip and innuendo" and accused *Newsday* of "publishing a long series of scurrilous attacks on the University." All of this was done to provide "an object lesson in how the liberal establishment responds to efforts to challenge its orthodoxies." Kimball adds that President Diamandopoulos's dream "that access to the full riches of a liberal education should be limited not by a student's 'modest means and modest learning' but only by his ambition, energy, and talent" has been frustrated by Adelphi's faculty: "lazy, more than 80 percent tenured, and exceptionally, indeed aggressively, mediocre." The President's aspirations for Adelphi makes them "nervous": "He wants to hold them to an intellectual and pedagogical standard higher than that to which they hold themselves."

Finally, Kimball explains why the editors of the *New York Times* entered the fray. They "remember what John Silber accomplished there [at Boston University] in the face of a similar barrage of criticism and misrepresentation.... They have never forgiven him for it, and they clearly will do everything in their considerable power to stop Peter Diamandopoulos from repeating his success at Adelphi." (Roger Kimball, "The Crusade against Adelphi," *Washington Times,* 17 November, 1995, p. A21).

12. See also *Vacco v. Diamandopoulos,* (and 17 other former Trustees), Sup Ct, New York County, 6 April, 1998, Ramos, J., Index No. 401253/97, New York County, Honorable Charles Edward Ramos, 6 April, 1998.
13. News Bureau Statement to the Media from Vince Passaro to Everyone, 18 April, 1996.
14. *Vacco v. Diamandopoulos,* There was apparently a great deal of merit to the attorney general's contentions as the University received an exceedingly favorable out-of-court settlement, on November 16, 1998, of all pending litigation and claims with regard to the University, and New York State.

Under the terms, the dismissed Trustees, other than Peter Diamandopoulos, refunded $800,000 for legal and other expenses incurred by the University; Diamandopoulos refunded $649,583 for excessive compensation, legal fees and other expenses; all of the Trustees, including Diamandopoulos, reimbursed the University an additional $225,000 for legal fees and other expenses; Adelphi's indemnity insurer refunded $1.45 million for legal fees; the former Trustees assumed responsibility for more than $400,000 in outstanding legal costs billed to the University and assumed responsibility of an action brought to recover some of those fees; Diamandopoulos relinquished his claim to the right to purchase the Manhattan apartment; after he was to vacate the apartment, Diamandopoulos would pay the University $106,000 ($5,000 a month for slightly over twenty-one months) for rent from February, 1997 through November, 1998; Diamandopoulos relinquished his claim for $411,000 in accrued sabbatical pay and $353,519 in accrued deferred compensation from his post-1993 contracts. (Amounts released to Diamandopoulos were recalculated based on his 1992-93 salary of $250,000 and deferred compensation of $50,000, which was deemed not excessive by the Board of Regents.)

In Diamandopoulos's counterclaim against Adelphi for breach of contract, the University agreed to pay $384,652 (this is 20 percent of his claim for salary minus the $98,500 annual salary as a professor of philosophy he had been receiving since he was removed as President) and to release to him $1.8 million in deferred compensation and interest—$1,015,199 from deferred compensation accounts, accrued by Adelphi prior to June, 1993, with financial earnings to October 9, 1998; $543,067 from deferred compensation accounts accrued under post-June, 1993 recalculated contracts at a rate of $50,000 per year; and $250,000 from accrued sabbatical accounts recalculated at 1/12 of a reduced annual salary. He also agreed to resign from the University.

The net gain to Adelphi from all of this was just over $4 million in cash and canceled debt, minus approximately $500,000 in legal fees to Adelphi's new lawyers. In the settlement, neither the former Trustees nor Diamandopoulos admitted any wrongdoing. This restoration of ill-spent funds, return of assets, and removal of accrued liabilities had no bearing on the reported $615,000 in legal expenses of the faculty's Committee to Save Adelphi, which was not a party to these actions. For some details and reaction to the agreement, see, David M. Halbfinger, "Settlement Reached in Suits on Ouster of Adelphi Chief," *New York Times,* 18 November, 1998, C24.

8

Conclusions

How Unique Is Adelphi and Its Governing Board?

Karl Marx drolly observed that "Hegel remarks somewhere that all facts and personages of great importance in world history occur, as it were, twice. He forgot to add: the first time as tragedy, the second as farce."[1] Actions taken by lay governing boards first at Sonoma State University and then at Adelphi University made it possible for Peter Diamandopoulos to "occur, as it were, twice." Perhaps because Diamandopoulos was of less-than-great importance, a good deal of what transpired during both of his presidencies was farce.

It is also relevant that the package of benefits the Adelphi Board bestowed on Diamandopoulos, while not standard, was not unique; nor were some of its other unusual actions. The Board provided Diamandopoulos with an outsized compensation package, guaranteed him cash payment for sabbatical leaves not taken, gave him a second residence, and, most importantly, acquiesced in all of his suggestions and decisions, no matter how unwise. The Board of Trustees of Boston University had earlier acted similarly with respect to its President, Adelphi Trustee John Silber, often referred to as Diamandopoulos's mentor.

There are other parallels between the Diamandopoulos and Silber presidencies. Each constantly quarreled, and indeed, seemed to relish confrontation, with a sizable number of faculty creating continuous turmoil on campus. Each formed close relationships with powerful Trustees who championed an array of administrative proposals and decisions. Each made exaggerated claims of having saved their institution from bankruptcy and certain demise.[2] At each school, former Trustees complained that they were forced off the Board for questioning or not fully supporting major or minor presidential initiatives and decisions, while, at the same time, other Trustees were involved in business transactions from which they derived substantial income. And there were widely publicized accusations and criminal investigations into alleged illegal activities on the part of the President and some Trustees at both Boston University and Adelphi University.

The Boards at Adelphi and Boston seemed to conduct their affairs in much the same manner:

> As several former school officials tell it, Silber was growing bored with his duties at BU [Boston University]. The quarterly meetings of the full board of trustees had degenerated into dog-and-pony shows, wherein members would pretend to thumb through thick, turgid reports, while committee chairs droned on about what an excellent job Silber was doing and what an excellent University BU had become.[3]

It is not unlikely that minutes of board meetings at Boston University during Silber's presidency would resemble the large sample of minutes of Board meetings from Adelphi, praising one and all, utilized in chapter 5.

Itself not singular or unique, what happened at Adelphi was surely extreme, but this does not mean that such willfulness on the part of an academic governing board and administration at the expense of faculty could not occur on other campuses. It can and does, but usually with fewer indiscretions and a good deal less venality. What must be remembered is that the root cause of the upheaval at Adelphi—the imbalance of power—is found on most campuses. If it was possible for the decade of sniping and scuffling to occur at Adelphi, it is possible for this to occur elsewhere.

The fact of lay governing boards pretty much assures that faculty will be overmatched when a governing board and administration working in tandem hatch some scheme. Boards need only take care not to overreach so as to catch the eye of civil authorities. The Adelphi faculty and the Committee to Save Adelphi did not force the Board of Trustees and President Diamandopoulos out; they merely exposed them. It was Diamandopoulos's and the Board's own actions that were responsible for their removal. It is unlikely that the Diamandopoulos administration and the Board that gave it life would have been dismissed if financial irregularities had not been unearthed and made public. That faculty may feel put upon is usually not enough to get a sympathetic hearing from anyone except other academics. As the New York State-appointed chair of the Adelphi Trustees recognized: "The official investigation occurred because media attention, marketplace pressures, and internal critique were not sufficiently powerful to alter or halt the harm being done to the University."[4] What was being done to faculty hardly mattered.[5]

The Adelphi case is best viewed in a broad context. By itself, the school is of no special import other than being the backdrop where a number of egregious and curious events took place. They happened not because Peter Diamandopoulos appeared to the Trustees to be an academic administrator from central casting or because he possessed the unfortunate combination of too high an opinion of his capabilities and an authoritarian streak. They took place because lay boards govern institutions of higher learning, and this effectively diminishes faculty power. Those with power can use it to attain their ends, good or bad, benign or ill-intentioned. With little power over resources, more often than not, faculty are unable to attain their ends—greater power over decision making and a larger share of an institution's resources; governing boards and the administrators they hire can more readily attain their ends than can faculty. They must only act within the law. This principle is obvious, and applies not only to institutions of higher learning.

Suggestions heard from time to time about what might be done to limit the problems lay governing boards too often create are usually ignored or precipitously rejected as idealistic extremism. No one's advice on the subject has been more straightforward than Thorstein Veblen's: "from the point of view of the higher learning, the academic executive and all his works are anathema, and should be discontinued by the simple expedient of wiping him off the slate; and that the governing board, in so far as it presumes to exercise any other than vacantly perfunctory duties, has the same value and should with advantage be lost in the same shuffle."[6] To most, however, Veblen's recommendations are seen as little more than a wry impracticality. Still, they do aptly call attention to what some governing boards do (and fail to do). Actually, in light of how some governing boards so badly stumble, they seem well grounded. At Adelphi, the duties of the Board were at most "vacantly perfunctory." Power had been ceded to the administration, consistent with the general drift in organizations in the twentieth century.

It is unclear what contributions lay governing boards make in furthering teaching or research in institutions of higher learning. True, it is often said that, if nothing else, they are necessary to serve as a buffer to protect a college or university from a restive public. In fact, trustees rarely act in this way. The Cold War years showed us how little they did to shield faculty in many American institutions of higher learning, and the institutions themselves, from preposterous and unfair political attacks.[7]

Some trustees are not only not actively supportive of the interests of the professoriate, but they would limit or take back what most faculty assume to be fundamental rights. For example, in his speech to the University community on freedom in America at Adelphi's centennial celebration, honorary Trustee William Simon observed,

> So, yes, we need more competition throughout America. We need parental choice and vouchers to revive healthy competition in our elementary and secondary schools, even though unions and education bureaucrats might not be happy.
>
> We need to eliminate tenure in our colleges and universities.
>
> We need to promote real enterprise in our cities.
>
> With full and unfettered freedom of competition, America can finally reach its full potential. And we will astound the world.
>
> But, without true competition, our cities will continue sliding toward third-world status.
>
> Our high schools will continue graduating students who can't read their diplomas or write intelligible English.
>
> And, colleges will grant diplomas to young men and women who may be well versed in multicultural curriculums, but who have little understanding of how free markets work.
>
> And, in columnist George Will's words, while teachers and professors who perpetuate this academic malpractice are often tenured and always comfortable, the students on the receiving end are always cheated and often unemployable.[8]

Simon is not the first trustee with an extreme political agenda that he would have an institution of higher learning and its faculty pursue.

To the administration's chagrin, but hardly surprising, this fusillade by Simon was greeted with derision—jeering, hissing, and general boisterousness—by many faculty in the audience. Simon's taunt reinforced the conviction of most faculty that among the Trustees there was little understanding of what higher education was all about and of daily life at Adelphi, and, in addition, that some lacked tolerance and compassion; the reaction reinforced the conviction of some Trustees that the Adelphi faculty needed guidance and discipline. For many, Simon's address was by far the most memorable event of the centennial festivities.

Valuing Governing Boards, and Defending Them

In his discussion of "the importance of boards," William G. Bowen contends,

> The exercise of collective responsibility through a board can slow down some kinds of decision making, but it can also dampen the enthusiasm of the aspiring autocrat. It provides checks and balances by adding layers of judgment and protections against abuse of powers and some forms of self-dealing, self-promoting, and favoritism.[9]

This is not necessarily true; the Board at Adelphi made the opposite of all of this possible.

The actions of lay governing boards reflect the constituencies they represent, which are often dominant economic and political interests not disposed to seeing faculty given more power, or much more of anything except possibly teaching. Some elites, among others, take for granted that the American professoriate is not only too lazy, but too liberal, even subversive, that it poses a danger to the social order. Some college and university trustees share this mistaken belief.

Even after wrongdoings had been proven, the Adelphi Board and President Diamandopoulos had a good number of supporters. The President of the Association of Governing Boards of Universities & Colleges succinctly articulated the most commonly expressed defense: "It troubles me that a quasi-governmental board or an attorney general could second-guess trustees in setting the compensation of a chief executive."[10] Like Bowen's misinstruction, this concern is nonsense: it fails to take into account that from the beginning of the inquiries by the Board of Regents and other New York State authorities there were indications of illegalities which would in the end prompt the (Republi-

can, relatively conservative, pro-business) attorney general to file a
29-count complaint against Diamandopoulos and seventeen other dismissed Adelphi Trustees to recover misspent funds, including legal
fees. (Adelphi would also ask the court to set aside the terms of
Diamandopoulos's contract and separation agreement.[11])

Not surprisingly, the institution of lay governing boards has more
supporters among academic administrators and others who wish to
continue to dominate American higher education than among faculty.
In response to the removal of the Adelphi Board of Trustees by the
New York State Board of Regents, Robert Atwell, a former college
president and president emeritus of the American Council on Education (a visible and relatively important organization representing academic organizations and administrations), writes that he was "troubled"
and "uneasy."[12] He is convinced "that the quality of appointees to
many public governing boards has deteriorated sharply in recent years,"
but does not believe that this is the case for private institutions. Without substantiation, he contends that: "As Clark Kerr and others have
so eloquently stated, the self-perpetuating governing boards at private
colleges and universities represent an important strength of American
higher education." At Adelphi, the Board surely represented an important weakness. Adelphi aside, whether lay governing boards are a
strength or a weakness remains an open question. Assertions that they
are one or the other do not make it so; research into the question
would probably show that most are adequate, some are good, and
some are not. Regardless of what might be found, it would still have
to be determined whether lay governing boards are truly necessary,
and whether institutions of higher learning would function better without them.

Atwell is undoubtably correct in concluding: "Most private-college
trustees take their oversight and stewardship responsibilities seriously
and do not exploit their institution for self-serving purposes." Even at
Adelphi this was true. There are no facts to suggest that the full Board
was involved in a criminal conspiracy. In a conversation, one of the
New York Regents most knowledgeable about higher education and
the Adelphi situation remarked, "It was clear to us [other Regents]
that a number of the Trustees were innocents; they may still [in the
early summer of 1999] not fully understand how they were used. This
should now be clear to you. It's been obvious to us almost since the
testimony began. They [these Trustees] really should be told this."

The Adelphi Trustees were dismissed not because they did not take their responsibilities seriously, but because too many did not fully understand what these responsibilities were, and they could not fully understand, because they, for the most part, did not understand academic culture. In the end, the Board was most concerned not with serving the University or the public, but with advancing the phantasms of President Diamandopoulos. It could only be said of a few that they "exploited the institution for self-serving purposes."

Atwell's views represent those of the bulk of trustees (not just a patronizing few like William G. Bowen), who assume that it is the faculty who are naive, greatly in need of corporate advice and everyday wisdom. This was hardly the case at Adelphi. The leadership of the dissident faculty may have had little institutional power, but it was practiced and merciless in making sure the faculty kept what it had. It was clearly too focused and self-righteous to be coerced by Diamandopoulos and his Board to surrender vested interests. A not inconsiderable number of academics know enough and care enough to be involved in managing colleges and universities. They may not be those with the best minds, but neither are those who pursue administrative careers.

Contrary to what is often said about those who believe it their duty to give no quarter to academic administrators—that they are gratuitously vicious or that they have found a diversion from an otherwise tiresome career—a good number seem attracted to academic politics because they would like to improve campus life, and believe that their efforts will maximize the learning of students. That is, they are much like academic administrators; some are ruthless, some are idealists.

The Adelphi case makes manifest the risk in following Atwell's elitist recommendation that the public would be best served by placing its "faith in the generally good judgment of governing boards." Events at Adelphi indicate that this remains risky.

Although all organizations have a good deal in common, there are elements that all do not share. The challenges encountered directing a manufacturing or commercial enterprise are not the same as those encountered directing a college or university. Particular knowledge about an educational institution and academic culture are needed in order to successfully govern a college or university. Adelphi did not have a department of classics or even one historian on the faculty with expertise in the ancient world. Yet, the Trustees, following President

Diamandopoulos's recommendation, readily pressed ahead with a mandatory curriculum built around courses focusing on the classical tradition. They were led to believe that by virtue of their graduate training, faculty are qualified and able to teach a wide range of undergraduate courses, even those in unrelated disciplines. Perhaps faculty should be able to do so, but graduate training is specialized and narrow and does not produce generalists. Graduate degrees are research degrees. No amount of bullying of a recalcitrant faculty will change this fact, regardless of how many members of a governing board find it economically unsound or unpalatable.

Finally, those accepting implicitly the view that oversight by the state or some other outside body does more harm than good hold a position that was advocated long before the founding of the United States.[13] Ironically, it was the exact opposite of this argument—that the only effective way to control faculty or students was with a body representing the public—first used to justify the institution of lay governing boards in American colleges and universities.

Atwell is just one of many who have expressed unhappiness with the inquiry and decision of the New York State Board of Regents. However, given what might have happened at Adelphi if there had been no oversight, some mechanism to protect institutions of higher learning from the whimsy, poor judgment, or wickedness of those charged with governing them seems appropriate. It is occasionally suggested that this would be an appropriate function for accrediting boards. However, these bodies presently do not have the authority, or, if they do, the will to use it. The Adelphi faculty's plea merely for some support from one such organization (the Middle States Association of Colleges and Schools) came to naught. Ensuring the common good is a governmental function. Institutions of higher learning should be no freer of the state's attention than organizations that sell apples or equities to the public, than those that trim our hair or our pets.

A View from Adelphi's New Board

The New York State-appointed chair of the Adelphi Trustees believes that its "most critical tasks" are the same as those of all boards: "to choose new presidential leadership and to assess the University's financial and academic conditions."[14] But the new Board is no more qualified to do this than its predecessor. The new chair, however, insists the Board has been successful, in large part, because it has "the cooperation of every component and every individual... above all, the relationships among the Trustees and with dedicated faculty, students, administration, staff, and alumni saved the University and set it on a new course." His pride is unqualified:

> What happened at Adelphi was, at one time, a bad story. Today, because of the Regents' actions and the ensuing events on our campus, the story is a good one. The University not only recovered, but it also is thriving.... The campus is energized with renewed confidence.

This reasoning rests on the assumption that individuals and not social arrangements primarily determine behavior, that outcomes are the results of intentions. Events at Adelphi during Diamandopoulos's presidency indicate a more complex picture. To begin with, Diamandopoulos's intentions—to provide a quality education to undergraduates—were admirable. The fact remains that the imbalance of power at Adelphi was not addressed, nor were problems resulting from the vagueness and instability of shared governance, matters considered in the concluding section.

To be sure, Adelphi is no longer in a state of crisis, but there is little evidence to conclude that the Board's selection of a new President was the best one. This judgment seems premature.[15]

Faculty Power: Professional Ideals

Academics are employees of organizations. Notwithstanding that they are professionals and by definition autonomous, this condition under which they must work implies some loss in the ability to control their work—what is done, how it is done, and its ultimate goal—in other words, a reduction of independence and discretion, defining characteristics of professionals. As Paul Starr has noted with reference to physicians: "By employing workers directly, an organization generally gains greater control over their behavior as well as the whole system of production. It can monitor worker performance more closely and exact greater compliance with its own goals. It can reorganize the process of production."[16] This also holds for academics.

While a profession may claim the right to set its own rules and standards, institutions of higher learning, as bureaucracies, have considerable control over all employees, professionals and nonprofessionals. Because "administrative authority is predicated on the control and coordination of activities by superiors [and] professional authority is predicated on autonomy and individual knowledge,"[17] there is an inherent strain in the relationship between academic administrators and faculty.

Academics are not the only professionals in need of a formal organizational structure to deliver their services. The military and the clergy face the same situation. Although this is a fundamental fact of how those who teach must work (except, of course, private tutors), it is still to be expected that the professoriate would attempt to minimize the loss of autonomy that comes with being employees in an organization.[18]

The professoriate has never come close to taking control of institutions of higher learning, although since the development of the American research university after the Civil War, segments of it have diligently worked to resist institutions of higher learning from taking more control of them. Success has been modest. The voices of those who have attempted to take their case to the public have often been drowned out by those with considerable influence over elites, lawmakers, the media, and opinion leaders.

For the most part, colleges and universities control the professoriate—and the academic profession. Academic authorities set salaries and teaching loads, decide how performance is evaluated, and have the final word in appointments and promotions. Those who, in addition to teaching, engage in research can sometimes do this independently of the college or university that employs them. They are therefore relatively freer from institutional constraints in their work than those who only teach. They can come closer to what Eliot Freidson sees as the core of professional status: "ultimate control over its own work.... Control over work need not be total: what is essential is control over the determination and evaluation of the technical knowledge used in the work."[19] This better describes someone who does research in addition to teaching than someone who only teaches. As Burton Clark has observed,

> Professionals who largely give advice or follow the guidelines of a received body of knowledge require extensive but not great autonomy for the individual and the group. They need sufficient leeway to give an honest expert opinion or to apply the canons of judgment of their field. Those requiring great autonomy are those who wish to crawl along the frontiers of knowledge, with flashlight or floodlight in hand, searching for the new—the new scientific finding, the new reinterpretation of history, the new criticism in literature or art.[20]

Moreover, because of the way the academic marketplace works, faculty involved in teaching and research have more employment options, and thus gain more autonomy than those who only teach. They also often hold appointments at more prestigious schools where the customs of faculty consultation and shared governance are more likely to have taken hold. It is almost axiomatic that the better a college or university, the more influence faculty have.[21] (This is one of the reasons why faculty members at these colleges and universities almost always reject unionism as a means to protect their interests. They may stand up to administrative authority, but are less likely to do so collectively.)

The visibility and bargaining power of active scientists and scholars reduce the probability that they would be subject to abuses experienced by the faculty at Adelphi. It is highly unlikely that what occurred at Adelphi could occur, for example, at Rice University or Oberlin College. Each has too many prominent faculty who could credibly invoke professional autonomy to resist administrative encroachments. Each has too many prominent alumni who would not hesitate to challenge the board and administration and apply economic pressure. Each has a set of traditions which dictate how board members, academic administrators, and faculty are to behave, relate to each other, and settle differences. To be sure, on occasion each might experience a scrum, but compromise in the attempt to resolve differences rather than the annihilation of an opponent generally informs the parties. The authorities and faculty of colleges and universities that want to be taken seriously in the academic world may not be able to prevent disagreements and conflict from erupting and being discussed where academics gather, but they can and do minimize being featured in the media by making concessions, and sincere attempts at resolution. More often than not, there is compromise and settlement. Diamandopoulos and his enemies on the faculty were unschooled in self-restraint, and can be faulted for not being willing to withdraw graciously. (In his determination to score points against his opponents, Diamandopoulos had apparently forgotten his Greek mythology and the fate of Daedalus's son Icarus who was not satisfied with simply escaping the labyrinth.)

Although diminished everywhere, there is great variation in faculty power among campuses. Still, it is important to bear in mind that most of the American professoriate teaches at institutions that more closely resemble Adelphi than they do Rice or Oberlin, that Adelphi is less unique than Rice or Oberlin. Like Adelphi, the majority of the 3,600-plus American colleges and universities are not selective of students (about 3 percent accept fewer than 50 percent of applicants; twice that number of schools accept over 90 percent), serve a local student body (most undergraduates attend schools within 100 miles of home; in 1995, the median distance traveled was 71 miles), do not have much of a reputation beyond the local region (unless they have successful Division I intercollegiate football or basketball programs), and have undistinguished faculty burdened with relatively heavy teaching loads. A large number are intellectual backwaters where faculty have never been recognized as professionals deserving of the smallest measure of autonomy. As long as faculty spend more time teaching than doing research and have few resources to fend off strong-willed administrators, efforts to change the imbalance of power on campus will likely founder. Faculty will continue to have relatively little power.

Academics are professionals, and some power comes with the status of being a professional. The claim of professional status works best for the charmed minority in academic life with high disciplinary prestige and visibility off campus. Through research, academics can display their knowledge. Starr, among others, has pointed out that knowledge can be "transformed into authority," and "authority into market power."[22] Engaging in research is a necessary condition for a more equal distribution of power. For the denizens of the bottom of the barrel the risks from an imperious board or academic administrator are considerable. (With more faculty on more campuses doing research, the barrel would be reshaped.)

All of this, in itself, should be a strong imperative for making it possible for faculty to engage in both teaching and research, so that only part of their professional lives is bound up in the college or university and part will be occupied with the details of scholarly rummaging. Faculty who would like to move in this direction should not expect help from most academic administrators in pursuing their scholarship. The latter may maintain that they would like faculty to do more research to bring research funds to campus and to enhance a school's reputation, but, for the most part they have little scholarly achievement, and, more importantly, are ambivalent about the prospect: they understand that professionally active faculty can be more independent than those who are not; they know that professionally active faculty will be less subject to the vicissitudes of institutional life.

If faculty were recognized as professionals and formally accorded greater power—beginning with more than token representation on governing boards—they could (ideally) redouble the efforts of institutions of higher learning to first and foremost pursue the goal of the higher learning. One contribution that any trustee might make is expertise. Presumably an academic as a board member would do that. And with most boards of colleges and universities having so long used co-option to fill their ranks, expertise might well be something that many could use. Whether more academics on boards would actually result in trustees being more independent of administrators is, of course, an open question. It would obviously depend on who the individuals were. The academics on the Adelphi Board were clearly at one with the administration.

Much has been made of the putative power of professionals, academics and others. Yet, as Philip Elliott cautioned over twenty-five years ago, "the professions have always occupied a marginal position in society, peripheral to the main divisions of class, status, power, and interest. This is still the case even though the professions have changed from being an addendum to the nobility and gentry to being part of the occupational elite in modern society.... The professions...fill the vacuum [of the primary basis of differentiation] in mass society, but this appearance can be challenged both on the grounds that they do not constitute a conscious, coherent elite group and that their grasp on power and rewards in society is limited and insecure."[23] This condition still holds.

Faculty Power: Shared Governance Revisited

Shared governance, by which faculty, the administration, and the governing board are expected to work together making decisions and policies, is nearly universal in American higher education. As a rule, faculty have most influence in helping to determine educational policies and procedures. (This principle may even be formalized, as it is at State University of New York: "The faculty of each college shall have the obligation to participate significantly in the initiation, development, and implementation of the educational program.")

Because of the haziness of the concept, an unusually large number of misunderstandings erupt in the attempt to implement shared governance. In one or another area, roles and functions can be specified, but often they are not. Lines of authority are sometimes blurred, making some—most often the least powerful, faculty—uncomfortable. This almost invariably produces tension. On some campuses, uncertainty and distrust are a constant. It is not uncommon for any act, consequential or innocuous, to be greeted with suspicion, and for a chill to overwhelm harmony. As the chair of the Board when Diamandopoulos was hired in 1985 remembered it, this was true at Adelphi from the time of his initial appointment as President:

James T. Byrne, Jr.:

Q: Now, before the offer was made to President Diamandopoulos, did you receive any faculty input with respect to his candidacy?

A: Yes, we did.

Q: What was the nature of that input?

A: I think—I believe it was a letter—it was either a memo or a letter that went to Board members—went to the Board, not Board members—went to the Board, and the substance of the correspondence—and I don't have copies of it—the substance of the correspondence was that they were concerned about our electing him to the presidency. In fact, it urged us not to give the presidency to Dr. Diamandopoulos because they had received correspondence or communications from Sonoma that he was a very difficult individual in terms of dealing with the faculty, and that he had denied tenure to faculty members at Sonoma, and that they thought that he was going to create problems at Adelphi and urged us not to appoint him.

Q: Did the Board discuss that?

A: Yes, the Board discussed it, and we made a decision that despite the concerns of the faculty, that we felt that he was the individual for the task at hand. (Testimony, pp. 5504-5)

Ten years later, the Trustees and President Diamandopoulos were not even troubling themselves to maintain the fiction of shared governance at Adelphi.

Currently, under ideal circumstances, shared governance is not the best arrangement. As often as not, it gives faculty an unrealistic feeling of power, that what they decide should or must count. An examination of a range of decisions over a period of time makes it obvious that this is not always the case. In some matters faculty—not only the faculty at Adelphi—may not even be consulted. (In one survey of faculty, on only two of eight items were more than 50 percent of the faculty critical of the performance of their governing board: "Board does not give serious consideration to faculty opinions." [61 percent]; "Arrangements are lacking for expression of faculty opinions within a system of shared governance.[50 percent][24]). Faculty too often forget that the president is appointed by and is an agent of the governing board, not of the faculty. Regardless of the degree of shared governance, there is an imbalance of power between the governing board/ administration and the faculty. The governing board delegates power; it can take it back if it deems it prudent to do so. The end result of attempts to work together is that many—not just faculty, but administrators and members of governing boards—become exasperated and disappointed; some become embittered. Some argue that there is too much democracy on campus, impeding the solution of pressing problems; some argue that there is too little, creating pressing problems.

It is difficult to imagine that it would be in the best interest of the public if faculty were granted complete autonomy. If not lay boards, someone is needed to protect the public from an autonomous faculty. At the same time, faculty must be given more than token power. This could begin by facing up to the fact that at present they have little. What is needed is true shared governance whereby faculty have clearly delineated responsibilities and authority that cannot be readily abrogated. Clearly, academic administrators need some power, but what they need to manage is a good deal less than what they now have. (In spite of the fact that they now have too much power, for some inexplicable reason, academic administrators incessantly complain that they have too little. One might wonder: for what purpose?)

However one views what is called shared governance as now conceived—as something that eviscerates effective leadership or as a cruel myth that serves to frustrate conscientious faculty—the friction it created at Adelphi reveals it to be much less than an unqualified good.

Notes

1. Karl Marx, *The Eighteenth Brumaire of Louis Bonaparte,* New York: International Publishers, 1963 (originally 1869), p. 15.
2. Diamandopoulos's questionable financial actions as an academic administrator were far from unprecedented. A treatise on the subject is overdue. The first head of Harvard College, Nathaniel Eaton, was charged not only with savagely beating his assistant, but also with fraudulent dealings that led to his indictment, dismissal from office, and eviction from colonial Massachusetts. (These facts certainly

make Diamandopoulos's advertising slogan, "Harvard, the Adelphi of Massachusetts," seem less inappropriate.)
3. John Strahinich, "The Fall of John Silber," *Boston Magazine*, Volume 85, Num-
    ber 6, June 1993, p. 105. One study identified "nine types of boards in terms of
    their overall orientation to their conduct." The Boards of Adelphi University and
    Boston University seem to typify the "out-to-lunch board" which "follows the
    recommendations of the president in an automatic way and, sometimes, has been
    deliberately stacked by the president (in private institutions) for the sake of this
    result. It usually goes along with or may give rise to a dominating president."
    (Clark Kerr and Marian L. Gade, *The Guardians: Boards of Trustees of American
    Colleges and Universities, What They Do and How Well They Do It,* Washington,
    DC: Association of Governing Boards of Universities & Colleges, 1989, p. 59).
4. Steven L. Isenberg, "Adelphi Postscript: The Restoration," *Trusteeship,* Volume
    7, Number 2, March/April 1999, p. 23.
5. This, of course, is not entirely true; some did express concern about the treatment
    of the faculty. In remarks to his colleagues, one Regent noted:

> The Trustees have ridden roughshod over the faculty rights in academic and
> educational affairs that are articulated in Governance Articles by permitting the
> administration to ignore faculty roles in appointments, curriculum, and courses;
> by supporting and collaborating in the cut-off of communications with the
> faculty; by withholding from faculty highly significant academic policy deci-
> sions.... The Trustees have abandoned many policy-making responsibilities to
> the President, and they have, together with the President, trampled on the rights
> of the faculty.(Saul B. Cohen, Comments to Regents, 10 February 1997).

6. Thorstein Veblen, *The Higher Learning in America: A Memorandum on the
    Conduct of Universities by Business Men,* New York: B.W. Huebsch, 1918, p. 286.
7. Lionel S. Lewis, *Cold War on Campus: A Study of the Politics of Organizational
    Control,* New Brunswick, NJ: Transaction Publishers, 1988.
8. William E. Simon, Remarks, Adelphi University's Centennial Celebration, 14
    September, 1995, pp. 11-12.
9. William G. Bowen, *Inside the Boardroom: Governance by Directors and Trust-
    ees,* New York: John Wiley & Sons, 1994, p. 1. Bowen is convinced that "man-
    agements of nonprofits simply could not survive on their own.... [Because they]
    reflect the interests of individuals who are idealistic [and] committed to a set of
    nonmonetary goals..., nonprofits need both the help and the stamp of approval
    that can be provided by the active presence on their boards of prominent business
    leaders, investors, lawyers, and statesmen." (p. 110). Quite obviously, Bowen
    would take issue with all or at least most of Veblen's observation that "Plato's
    classic scheme of folly, which would have the philosophers take over the man-
    agement of affairs, has been turned on its head; the men of affairs have taken over
    the direction of the pursuit of knowledge. To any one who will take a dispassion-
    ate look at this modern arrangement it looks foolish, of course,—ingeniously
    foolish...." (Veblen, pp. 77-78).
        Veblen was disheartened that the industrialists and other men of affairs, who
    since the Civil War had begun to dominate university governing boards, were in a
    position to completely impose their pecuniary values on the world of scholarship
    and science. This problem has become more evident in the later decades of the
    twentieth century than in the earlier ones. Here is the explanation of one Trustee
    of why he pressed for sizable benefits for President Diamandopoulos:

Abraham Krasnoff:

Q [from Regent]: Do you recall any specific discussions about the deferred compensation issue, as part of this dialogue?

A: As I said a minute ago, that was a major part of this dialogue: How does one assure somebody in his mid-sixties enough incentives—not that he was, didn't appear to have incentive, but nevertheless—since I was something older than the mid-sixties at that point, I lived through the process, and the idea of providing long-term incentive compensation which happened to me in my own career, and to me, this was a good idea.

Q: Did you articulate your sense of this?

A: Of course, I did.

Q: What did you tell fellow Board members?

A: I told them that this happened with me, I was a long-term CEO, and I suppose people were interested in insuring I was going to be there. But for whatever reason, when I was something past sixty, I recall it, I was granted a long-term deferred compensation arrangement. Although mine was not tied to the necessity to be on the job; mine accrued and was there whether I stayed or not. But we wanted to tie him down.

Q: Based on your experience—well, first, other than your own personal experiences with your own compensation and with the compensation of Pall Corporation—what other experience or insights on compensation did you bring to this dialogue?

A: Well, you know, I guess we all come at events from our own background. My background is in dealing with—I mentioned the American Business Conference yesterday, where I was in close contact with a hundred leaders of mid-size growth companies, many of them people who engineered turnarounds or people who, having engineered turnarounds, having continued success. But my experience is that's what you reward. I think that's the experience of the world, generally, but that's my experience; you reward turnarounds and continued financial success after turnarounds. (Testimony, pp. 6589-90)

The majority of Trustees were convinced that it was their business experience that qualified them to serve on the Board. Their pragmatism informed most decisions, even one that led them to deceive faculty about plans to retrench academic programs.

James T. Byrne, Jr.:

A: I wasn't concerned about ruffling feathers, but I certainly was concerned about a mass exodus, okay, and I can only draw on my own experience in business.

I mean, if we start looking at a particular subsidiary in a company, and we start raising questions at the Board level as to whether that subsidiary on a long-term basis fits into the overall strategy, we are not going to issue a press statement that day saying that this no longer fits, because you can just about shut it down at that point, it's dead.

Q [from Regent]: Then you regard the digest of the Master Plan or the Academic Plan that went to the faculty as a kind of a press statement?

A: No. (Testimony, pp. 5343-44)

10. Quoted in Karen W. Arenson, "Educators Differ on College Trustees' Activities and Ethics," *New York Times,* 15 February, 1997, p. 28.
11. As was noted in chapter 7, all were accused of waste, mismanagement, imprudence, and neglect. In addition, Diamandopoulos was charged with having amassed "an unreasonable compensation package" and two Trustees were charged with having failed to inform the Board that businesses with which they were associated were not providing services to the University free of charge. (See chapter 7, note 14, for the terms of the out-of-court settlement.)
12. Robert H. Atwell, "After Adelphi: Insuring That Private Colleges Remain Faithful to the Public Interest," *Chronicle of Higher Education,* 7 March, 1997, p. B6.
13. This belief has been fed by tenets of American thought which hold that government is dangerous and a threat to freedom, that those who are part of government have poorer judgment than those who are not, and that the government is less efficient and effective than the private sector.
14. Isenberg, "Adelphi Postscript," pp. 23-24.
15. Although he signed a five-year contract, the President the Board settled on resigned in the summer of 1999, after a year of service, to take a better position, suggesting that he was more interested in his own career than he was in Adelphi's students.
16. Paul Starr, *The Social Transformation of American Medicine,* New York: Basic Books, 1982, p. 26.
17. Robert Birnbaum, *How Colleges Work: The Cybernetics of Academic Organization and Leadership,* San Francisco: Jossey-Bass, 1988, p. 10.
18. Moreover, Freidson has reminded us,

That he has been an employee for centuries has not left the professor without important freedom. Control over the terms and conditions of work is certainly weakened by being an employee rather than an entrepreneur in a favorable marketplace. Nonetheless, control over the *content* of work is not at all necessarily so weakened. (Eliot Freidson, "Professions and the Occupational Principle," in Eliot Freidson, Editor, *The Professions and Their Prospects,* Beverly Hills, CA: Sage, 1973, p. 36).

19. Eliot Freidson, *Profession of Medicine: A Study of the Sociology of Applied Knowledge,* New York: Dodd, Mead, 1970, pp. 185-86.
20. Burton R. Clark, "Faculty Organization and Authority," in Terry F. Lunsford, editor, *The Study of Academic Administration,* Boulder, CO: Western Interstate Commission for Higher Education, 1963, p. 43.
21. Lionel S. Lewis, *Marginal Worth: Teaching and the Academic Labor Market,* New Brunswick, NJ: Transaction Publishers, 1996.
22. Starr, *Social Transformation,* p. 144.
23. Philip Elliott, *The Sociology of the Professions,* New York: Herder and Herder, 1972, p. 143.
24. Kerr and Gade, *The Guardians,* table B-11, p. 174.

Index